Xi Jinping's Governance and the Future of China

Zhou Xinmin
Foreword by Latha Ramchand
Preface by Fu Chengyu

Skyhorse Publishing

Skyhorse Publishing books may be purchased in bulk at special discounts for sales promotion, corporate gifts, fund-raising, or educational purposes. Special editions can also be created to specifications. For details, contact the
Special Sales Department, Skyhorse Publishing, 307 West 36th Street, 11th Floor, New York, NY 10018 or info@skyhorsepublishing.com.

www.skyhorsepublishing.com

10 9 8 7 6 5 4 3 2 1

Library of Congress Cataloging-in-Publication Data is available on file.

Print ISBN: 978-1-5107-3622-1
eBook ISBN: 978-1-5107-3628-3

Cover design by Brian Peterson

Printed in the United States of America

Contents

Publisher's Disclaimer

This book by Zhou Xinmin comes to us translated into English from Chinese. In editing the manuscript, Skyhorse has done its best to remain faithful to the translation in order to avoid changing the meaning or intent of the book.

Author's Bio

Zhou Xinmin, who created the theory of leaders' core ca
pabilities in China, is also a well-known expert in the research of Chinese leadership. He is the author of *Core Capabili-
ties-Understanding These Three Years of Governing, Leaders' Core
Capabilities, Leaders' Core Capabilities of State-owned Enterprises*
(Chinese and English Edition), *Evaluation and Practice of Leaders' Core Capabilities of State-owned Enterprises, Core Capabili-
ties-107 Questions about How to Shape Leadership*, and *Achieving
China Dream with the Core Capabilities-A Collection of Interview
Records.*

FOREWORD

Great leaders build lasting organizations. Leadership of a nation, especially that of a vast country like China, calls for strategic and tactical skills at every level of the organization. As organizations grow, so do the challenges in communicating the leader's philosophy and converting it into organizational capabilities. Hence, intentional efforts to permeate the leadership culture across all members is critical to success. Zhou Xinmin's latest book, *Xi Jinping's Governance and the Future of China*, is set against this background. The book unpacks the core tenets of President Xi's governance philosophy and uses them to provide a road map to Communist Party of China leaders who must convert the belief systems into action. All CPC leaders will benefit from Xinmin's insight into President Xi's leadership. The book also serves as a useful guide to global leaders who can benefit from understanding the perspective that President Xi brings to international conversations. Xinmin's work combines theoretical with practical aspects of leadership and is a must read for anyone doing business in and with China. As Dean of the C.T. Bauer College of Business, I am doubly proud of the contribution of Zhou Xinmin who is an alum of the institution.

Latha Ramchand
Dean and Professor, Finance
C.T. Bauer College of Business
University of Houston

PREFACE

Over the past few years, growing attention has been paid to the changes that are quietly reshaping China and to the governance philosophies of Xi Jinping, its new steersman. Since the 18th National Congress of the Communist Party of China in 2012, the new generation of China's leadership headed by Xi has been pressing the Chinese Dream forward with an unparalleled level of resolve and political wisdom. A new era is on the horizon to witness the rejuvenation of the Chinese nation. For its many achievements, the Chinese leadership enjoys the love and support of the Chinese people, and has won wide acclaim around the globe.

In a few years' time, President Xi has developed his philosophical thinking on the governance of China into a system to address the pressing issues of China, to develop and improve Chinese socialism, and to achieve modernization in all areas. His ideas also contain the guiding principles for building a new world order and influencing the future of human society.

Studying, understanding, and implementing these philosophies on governance is a pressing political task of the CPC and the nation. Only by fully understanding these philosophies can we apply them in our work. This will not be an easy task for it requires the whole Party to put in extra effort.

Zhou Xinmin's new book, *Xi Jinping's Governance and the Future of China*, explains the characteristics and patterns of President Xi's governance philosophy from the perspective of core capabilities required of the Chinese leadership. This book can also serve as a reference to help CPC members and officials absorb and internalize key concepts.

In recent years, as the education campaign rolls out to study President Xi's speeches and thoughts, interpretations in various forms have been made available in the market. Compared to previous works, this book has something new to offer. It has moved away from literal interpretation in a general sense, and employs a new perspective to focus on core capabilities—the supporting element behind governance philosophies—to conduct an in-depth analysis that is accessible and comprehensive.

There is no doubt that with more practice, the philosophical system will continue to develop and improve while enriching its contents. The essential capabilities of leadership, the decisive and fundamental pillars of the system, will not change with the times. This book explains the achievements, strategies, and development of the president's governance practice, and showcases the vision and capacities of the new generation of CPC leadership. This will undoubtedly help readers and Chinese officials at all levels in understanding President Xi's thoughts.

Theories are meant to guide practice, therefore we must understand these theories before implementing them in the key strategies and policies of the CPC and the state, and use them to guide our action. With this book in hand, CPC members and officials will find it easier to understand the principles and key concepts, and use it as a guidebook to measure their performance against the president's standards. Officials must study and practice these rules, continue to enhance their capacities, and perform their duties in a way that follows the example of the leadership in national governance.

Divided into seven chapters, this book builds upon the main theme of capabilities and employs a step-by-step approach in detailing its meaning with clear logic and rigorous deduction. Chapter 1, Achievements of Xi Jinping's Practice of Governance, offers a comprehensive account of the CPC leadership's governance philosophies, measures, and accomplishments.

Chapter 2, Interpreting Xi Jinping's Governance Philosophies, makes an in-depth analysis of the guiding thoughts. Chapter 3, Practice of Xi Jinping's Governance Philosophies, discusses the policies and methods employed. Chapter 4, The Governance of Great Leaders, summarizes the common traits of outstanding leaders. Chapter 5, Core Capabilities of Xi Jinping's Governance, analyzes President Xi's competence as China's leader. Chapter 6, Development of Xi Jinping's Governance Capabilities, traces back to the origin of Xi's capabilities and follows his developmental path. Chapter 7, Setting Standards for Leading Capabilities, explores the values extended from the capabilities of national governance. It is my hope that, by discussing these theories, the book will play a central role in influencing and molding generations of CPC members and officials who are committed to CPC's mission, Chinese socialism, and the rejuvenation of the Chinese nation. It is also my hope that it will help the modernization of China's governance system and capabilities, and shed some light on achieving the Chinese Dream.

Karl Marx once said, "Every beginning is difficult." The research on President Xi's governance philosophies is in its initial stage, with very few studies on the supporting capabilities behind the system. As a pioneer in this area, the author explains his original ideas in this work, some of which are yet to be tested through practice. I genuinely hope that the book will become the centerpiece in the education campaign on governance for CPC members and officials, and that it will enhance the implementation of President Xi's thinking on governance in China.

Fu Chengyu
February 22, 2016

INTRODUCTION

Capabilities of Leadership—Call of the Times

Since the 18th National Congress of the Communist Party of China (CPC) in 2012, the CPC central leadership led by Xi Jinping has been pressing reform forward in all areas by introducing new policies in governing the nation, the CPC, and the military. It has managed domestic development and Chinese foreign relations with a global vision, driven reform to a deeper level, and launched a new voyage of the People's Republic of China (PRC) towards prosperity. A new era has begun for both CPC's mission and for the renewal of China.

Over the past few years, we have witnessed remarkable progress in China's governance. The achievements and progress in governance have never been so evident. These achievements have given the Chinese people new hope, new aspirations, and new dreams. The expectation is that over the next few years, and the years that follow, China will make even greater progress in its reform and development and that the CPC will continue to consolidate its foundation of governance, explore new heights of governance, continue to make the Chinese proud, and leave the world in wonder.

In China, the drastic changes and achievements since the 18th National Congress of the CPC in 2012 are closely related to the collective leadership of the CPC, especially of President Xi. With his political vision, pioneering spirit, governance wisdom, leadership skills, and personal qualities, he has quickly won the support of the Party and the people since he took charge of the CPC, the state, and the military. He is known for his philosophies on governance, his resolve and determination, and his charisma in effectively governing China and promoting overall development. Under his strong leadership, the CPC and the country have undergone profound changes. For his central role, President Xi has won the support and love of over a billion Chinese people.

President Xi's influence goes beyond China's borders. He has been listed six times in TIME 100, an annual list of the 100 most influential people in the world. He has been hailed as "the most transformational Chinese leader since Deng Xiaoping," "the-leader of a rising China," and "China's first truly global leader." Some international organizations and well-known media outlets have also praised Xi's governance practice, with great expectations for China's future. It is commonly believed that Xi Jinping will "bring China long-term prosperity and stability through revitalizing China's economy and improving people's well-being;" that he will "continue to improve the governance of the CPC and the country, solve China's problems at deeper levels, establish a new mode of sustainable development, and eventually boost China's international competitiveness." He will "build a new type of international relations focusing on cooperation and reciprocity, play the part of a leader of a responsible country, and build a brand new international image for China." We have reason to believe that with the development of his governance philosophy and practice, and with new achievements and growing influence, Xi will become an outstanding leader who will influence the future of China and the world.

Currently, many institutes and organizations around the globe are studying Xi's governance style and philosophies in order to probe into China's future direction, potential, and developmental trends. This reflects the global attention on China's development and is also inspired by Xi's charisma as a state leader. It is of strategic and realistic significance to dig into the essence of Xi's governance wisdom, to summarize and apply his philosophies in our work, and to understand the nature of his thinking through logical reasoning. First, it will be conducive to introducing the political beliefs and pursuits of the CPC, and the theoretical basis and institutional advantages of China's path of socialism, to show the world why the CPC can succeed in terms of political leadership. Second, it will be conducive to showcasing the vision, ambition, and charisma of the leadership of the CPC, with Xi Jinping as the leader, to explain why he is competent as China's leader—to the people of China, and to the world. Third, it will be conducive to setting the standards for essential capacities, so that officials in China can fully understand and implement the decisions of the CPC Central Committee on state, Party and military governance, that they can help improve the CPC's governance ability, modernize the governance system and capacity, realize the Chinese Dream with newly mustered strength, and that they can continue to succeed alongside Xi. Also, as a leading figure connecting all of China, Xi and his theories will undoubtedly become a key component of the theoretical foundation of Chinese socialism, and a key accomplishment of applying Marxism in China. With further summation at the theoretical level, the theories will play a major role in innovating the existing theoretical system.

Leadership capabilities are a new and pioneering theory of contemporary leadership. The theory contends that the essential capabilities of leaders play a central role in the development of an organization or a nation. They are the backbone of the ability to lead, the fundamental, directional, and crucial link of the entire system of leadership capabilities, and the basis for any leader to perform his function as a steersman of his country's development. The system of leadership capabilities is composed of two levels: the leading capabilities for top leaders and for middle- and high-level leaders. The leading capacity, at the top level, is the basis of the system, which is supported by the capabilities at the middle-level. They are closely connected to each other and support each other. In China, the leaders at all levels are required to have the "hard" capacities and "soft" capacities, which have gone beyond the traditional sense of "leading ability." Under the new criteria, officials must have the required level of political conviction, leadership skills, innovative spirit, and ethics and morality. Covering all categories and easy to understand, the new criteria are highly concise with emphasis on specific areas, and are quantifiable and assessable as a theoretical tool based on previous experiences and current conditions. By applying the theory of leadership capabilities, we will be able to identify and train outstanding officials, develop a system to govern officials and share it with the rest of the world. Based on the capabilities theory, this book carries an in-depth study of President Xi's speeches, strategies, and measures on governance, in an effort to summarize the capabilities of Xi, and to share his vision, charisma, wisdom, and original philosophies with readers around the world. By building a system of capabilities at the central leadership, the CPC will be able to set the standards of outstanding leadership for officials at all levels. With the right direction, officials can improve themselves in terms of capacities. In this way a solid organizational foundation will be established for achieving the Chinese Dream.

CHAPTER ONE

Achievements of Xi Jinping's Practice of Governance

Key Points

From 2012 to 2016, Xi has made major achievements in six areas:

- Completing the building of a moderately prosperous society in all respects
- Transforming and upgrading the growth model
- Driving reform to a deeper level
- Combating corruption, implementing the rule of law, and creating a new political ecology
- Thoroughly implementing Party discipline
- Increasing the use of diplomacy to create a new world order

It was after China entered the new stage of reform and development that Xi Jinping took over to lead the CPC with other members of the leadership. His appearance as the leader of the new central leadership attracted widespread attention domestically and globally due to the people's new aspirations, the new stage of reform and development, and the new changes in international politics and the economy. The world wanted to know what kind of vision and wisdom Xi would exhibit to steer

China, the ancient ship that has set sail in new waters, and what kind of strategy and governance skills he would exhibit to lead the Chinese people towards revitalization and prosperity.

It was amazing how quickly Xi took on his role as the steersman, and led the new leadership to begin a new voyage with courage and resolve. Carrying forward the revolutionary spirit of Mao Zedong, Deng Xiaoping and other leaders from earlier generations, Xi has exhibited the capacity and vision to govern China in the new age. His call for expanding the reform and progress in governance has ushered in a new era, leading the CPC and China in its aim to build a more prosperous society, to carry reform to deeper levels, to implement the rule of law, and to strengthen CPC discipline. Since 2012, he has fully demonstrated his ability to do these things.

It is evident that in these few short years, Xi Jinping's achievements in governance were reflected in all areas and sectors, and at all levels: completing the building of a moderately prosperous society, transforming and upgrading the growth model, driving reform to a deeper level, combating corruption, implementing the rule of law and a new political ecology, increasing Party discipline, and increasing the use of diplomacy to create a new world order.

I. The Building of a Moderately Prosperous Society in All Respects

Achievements
- Concept enriched
- Development coordinated
- Concrete steps taken

The building of a moderately prosperous society, in all respects, is a strategic plan of the CPC based on contemporary China's conditions and stage of development and is an important step to realizing the Chinese Dream. Once the mission is completed, there will be qualitative change in Chinese society. The new goal of emphasizing prosperity is to be accomplished in all respects, including politics, economics and culture, to meet the demands of both urban and rural development. This goal is testimony to the courage of the CPC, which has made a solemn promise to the Chinese people, and provided a timetable for completing the mission.

Since late 2012, the new generation of CPC's leadership has taken action to implement the decisions and plans approved at the 18th National Congress, by enriching governance philosophies and promoting the building of "a moderately prosperous society in all respects." The prosperity goal has been made a top priority in a Four-Pronged Strategy. Since the Congress, the CPC has made new achievements in this regard and in the meantime has gained substantial experience.

Achievement one: concept enriched

In terms of content, the prosperity goal targets the areas of economics, politics, culture, society and ecology with a comprehensive approach. In terms of scope, it covers all regions of China, and aims to eradicate poverty in the country by 2020. In terms of criteria, the standard of "moderate prosperity," a dynamic index, will change as the economy and society develop, and is expected to be on the rise. As the concept and contents continue to be enriched, the people have a clear direction and a road map for the mission, and are better prepared to take action.

Achievement two: development coordinated

Under the Four-Pronged Strategy, efforts to complete the building of a "moderately prosperous society in all respects" have been coordinated and mutually enhanced in the areas of economics, politics, culture, society, ecology, and Party building.

In the economic sector, China has entered a New Normal, featuring steady growth, transforming growth model, developing high-end industries, consumption-driven growth, and industrial upgrading. In politics, under CPC leadership, achievements have been made in promoting political democracy, implementing the rule of law, supervising officials, and fighting against corruption to develop a sound political ecology. In the cultural sector, the charm of Chinese culture is felt around the globe, and China's soft power is on the rise. In the social sector, new progress has been made in defending the rights and interests of the people, safeguarding social fairness and justice, and improving people's well-being. In the area of ecology, answering the call to build a more beautiful China, more people have begun to respect nature and follow its natural laws. People are living greener lives, and energy conservation and environmental protection have become basic national policies. In Party building, Party discipline has been strengthened, and CPC members and officials are setting good examples for the people. Cohesiveness, unity, and strength of the CPC have been enhanced. The coordinated development of all areas has built valuable experience for handling tough problems and given the Chinese confidence in their ability to complete goals.

Achievement three: concrete progress made

It is the people who can judge whether they are living a good life, and it is the people who constitute the foundation of the nation. Over the past three plus years, China took people's well-being as a central task, and rested prosperity in all respects on the foundation of sufficiency in the material sense. Among the tasks decided at the Third Plenary Session of the CPC's 18th Central Committee, several dozen were about people's well-being, including areas such as healthcare, education, employment, and housing, which are closely related to people's interests and are of pressing concern for the people. China has pushed forward reforms designed to improve living standards with unprecedented fortitude and intensity, achieving a series of solid accomplishments that the people can see, feel, and benefit from. The reform of wealth distribution has been initiated, and an olive-shaped income-distribution structure is being formed. The reform of the household registration system is being implemented. Registered households in different key cities are getting treated more equally, and rural registered residence will become a thing of the past. Some students are now allowed to take the college entrance examination where they choose to study rather than at the schools of their registered residences, and more students from rural areas will be enrolled in key universities. Supervision of food security will be coordinated and enhanced, to ensure food safety. Medical insurance will cover more categories of diseases, and the urban-rural gap will be narrowed in terms of medical care standards. Policies of precisely targeted poverty reduction, with close management of the recipients, projects, funding, measures, sending of officials, and effects, will be implemented. A new round of decrepit area renovation has begun, and poverty reduction efforts are being focused on "poverty belts" where entire regions of people are struggling under the poverty line. Ecological recovery projects, represented by the Yangtze River project, have been launched to promote the productivity of ecological products and safeguard people's environmental rights. In 2014 alone, 13 million new jobs were created in urban areas, and the national per capita disposable income reached 20,167 yuan, growing faster than the GDP. The basic retirement pension has increased for nine consecutive years, the subsidies for the new rural cooperative medical system have kept increasing, and the social security network is covering more people. A total of 7.4 million units of low-income housing began construction in urban areas, and 2.66 million dilapidated houses in rural areas were renovated. The fruits of development are benefiting every Chinese citizen, and the people's wish for a good life is becoming reality. The Chinese are living happier lives.

II. Transforming and Upgrading the Growth Model

Achievements
- New economic theories developed
- Hardships and progress
- A bright future for Chinese economy

The economy is the basis of a country's strength and the lifeline of its development. In the last few years, China's economy has exhibited new traits: growth has slowed down to a more sustainable rate; with the upgrading of the economic structure, tertiary industry is now serving the majority of consumption demands; and the economic engine, which was powered by production factors, is increasingly driven by innovation, and is promoting the role of the market and releasing the vitality of reform. These changes demonstrate that China's economy has officially entered a new stage of development and a New Normal featured by structural adjustment, transformation and upgrading. These past few years witnessed great changes in China's development philosophy, growth model, and growth engine. Painful as it has been, the process has been effective and the results are positive.

Achievement one: development of new economic theories

Faced with the problems accumulated during China's 30-plus years of high-speed growth and the adverse impacts of the global financial crisis, Xi Jinping made a timely analysis of China's economic problems on deeper levels and correctly judged the economic situation in the current stage of development. He defined development as "well-balanced development conforming to the laws of economics," and "sustainable development following the laws of nature." On this basis, Xi developed his own economic theories surrounding the Chinese Dream and covering the following areas: the dominant role of socialist public ownership, the people's well-being and other fundamental questions regarding the Chinese economy, transforming the growth model and improving development and innovation, obtaining a deeper understanding of China's economic pattern and innovation of the economic philosophy, and improving China's model of economic governance.

The new economic theories are developed in light of China's conditions, and will guide the long-term development of China's economy by following several key concepts. The first economic strategy should aim at realizing the Chinese Dream. The Chinese Dream will only come true after China completes the building of a "moderately prosperous society in all respects," which will require many concrete tasks and steps. Accomplishing this level of prosperity will require clear goals and action plans. A timetable has been set for step-by-step implementation of these plans to fulfill the people's aspirations. The second economic strategy should aim at steady progress. This thinking has been able to prevent local governments from blind pursuit of GDP targets and disorderly expansion. It has prevented governments from financing vanity projects, and is conducive to helping officials foster the correct attitude towards political performance. The third economic strategy should aim at improving people's lives. By adopting the concepts of Gross Domestic Product of Welfare and Happiness Index, President Xi will be able to reinforce the principle of common prosperity, a cornerstone of Chinese socialism, and let every person enjoy the benefits of development equally. The fourth economic strategy should aim at upholding the dominant role of socialist public ownership. The privatization of State-Owned Enterprises (SOEs), of land and finance—signs of neoliberalism—were eliminated and its adverse impacts eliminated. The fifth economic strategy should aim at promoting urban-rural integration. President Xi is committed to solving the issues facing agriculture, farmers and rural areas, which are constraining comprehensive development at their root. The equal exchange of urban and rural production factors and the balancing of public resources will give voice to social fairness and justice to the largest possible extent. The sixth economic strategy should aim to promote innovation- and technology-driven growth. Scientific innovation and institutional innovation, two pillars for progress in contemporary China, will be reinforced as China's core competitiveness for national prosperity. The seventh economic strategy should aim to integrate overall development with local development. By collectively handling the relationship between overall advancement and key progress, and between top-level design and reform, development, and stability, President Xi is able to hold to a well-balanced outlook on development, a dialectical view of reform, and to prevent fundamental mistakes and disastrous errors. The eighth economic stratefy should aim at supply-side reform. By promoting structural adjustment through reform, the quality and efficiency of the supply system will be enhanced, the economy will continue to grow with good momentum, and social productivity will step up to a higher level.

Achievement two: concrete progress in economic transformation amidst hardships

Since late 2012, the new generation of the CPC's central leadership has been holding onto the bottom line of economic development, with clear strategic positioning, accurate understanding of the development trend, innovative adjustments of the guiding thoughts, calm responses to downward pressure, and the resolve to push forward economic transformation. During this period, China has made solid progress at times of hardship, and a firm foundation has been laid for the long-term development of the country's economy. The last few years of practice has proven that China's economy is more stable at a seven percent growth rate. Facing a new situation and new problems under the New Normal, China did not blindly print money or expand its investments, which would have only resulted in a deficit. Instead, it tapped its idle assets, enabling its economy to heal and adjust. Further adjustment has been made in the economic structure. Consumption now contributes more to economic growth than investment does, the added value of the service industry is increasing at higher rates than the manufacturing industry, and new technology and equipment manufacturing are growing faster than the average industrial growth rate, with quality development as the key. Resident income is taking up more room in income distribution, and energy consumption per GDP continues to decline, showing significant improvement in development quality. On the roles of the market and the government, both the "invisible hand" and the "visible hand" have played their roles, complementing and promoting each other for integrated and balanced development. The change of government functions and active performance of the market have inspired ordinary people to start up businesses in various capacities. More growth points are emerging, new growth forces are accelerating and accumulating strength, and the unbalanced economic system is being overturned towards one in favor of better, internally-driven growth.

Achievement three: progress in economic transformation heralding a bright future

Over the past few years, the journey of economic transformation has not been easy, the results not completely satisfactory, and expectations might not be fully fulfilled. Despite all of this, achievements were made by implementing new thoughts and exploring new paths; they were realized amidst the global economic downturn and complex geopolitical circumstances, and in the most difficult conditions as China drives its reform to a deeper level. It is fair to say that these accomplishments are more valuable than gold and reflect the resolve, courage and tenacity of the Chinese leadership to uproot institutional illnesses for future development. We have reason to believe that as soon as China makes it through the current stage, it will have a new beginning and will be rewarded handsomely. More than a few years of practice has demonstrated that China's economy, in the pursuit of well-designed, healthy and sustainable development, is vigorous and has a bright future. Domestically, the New Normal means new challenges, but also opportunities, in the following senses: First, despite slower growth rates, the size of the economy will continue to grow under a more sustainable growth model. Second, steadier growth will bring about more channels of power engines. Third, an upgraded economic structure promises more chances and ample room for development. Fourth, the streamlining of administration and delegation of powers to lower levels will release the vitality of the market. Just as Xi Jinping analyzes, despite slower growth rates, China's economy is still tenacious and has great potential. China still has a strong economic foundation and favorable conditions for growth, and economic restructuring and upgrading will continue to advance the economy.

Internationally, the transformation of the Chinese economy has brought opportunities to the global economy in the following senses: One, China's economy will maintain middle-to-high-speed growth, and will pull the world out of the economic downturn. Two, the consumption potential released from China's economic transformation will drive the global economy. Three, the Belt and Road Initiative (B&R) will provide unprecedented opportunities for the 65 nations included, and create a new model of regional economic development underlined by mutual benefit and common prosperity. Four, China's economic transformation will push the global industrial chain up the ladder and upgrade global industries.

It is well-expected that China, now and in future, will undoubtedly develop its economy to a more sophisticated state with improved labor division and structure. Under the New Normal, the Chinese economy will chart a new path of development with higher quality and efficiency, better structure, and more advantages, to reward the Chinese people and surprise the world.

III. Driving the Reform to a Deeper Level

Achievements
- Reform road map set by top-level design
- Reform of the economic system
- Reform benefits distributed in an orderly fashion

After three decades of reform and opening-up, China has achieved significant results that are acknowledged globally. The reform is still ongoing. Now that the easier tasks are completed, the reform will be pushed to deeper levels to tackle more difficult problems. This signifies that China's new round of reform has entered a "deep-water zone" of the toughest tasks, the target areas are intertwined and the involved groups are competing with each other. Institutional reform must be carried out to lead the breakthrough. Since 2012, the new generation of CPC leadership has, with great political courage and a strong sense of mission, broken into the "forbidden" zones of reform, initiating a new wave of reform in all respects and at deeper levels. As new benefits are being released, Chinese people have also opened up their minds and become more creative.

Achievement one: top-level design setting the road map to deeper reforms

To liberate and develop the productive forces and to adjust the superstructure to the economic base, the CPC leadership has strengthened top-level design to clarify the reform goals, guidelines, and methods. Its role of guidance can be reflected through different aspects. To begin with, the CPC Central Leading Group for Overall and Further Reforms was established to oversee the overall designing, planning and coordination, and implementation of the reforms. Secondly, new thinking has been developed to guide the reforms, emphasizing the necessity to pursue further reform if China wants to progress. Thirdly, the reform goals have been set: to create an environment for fair competition, to enhance the vitality of the economy and the society, to improve government efficiency and functions, to realize social fairness and justice, to promote social harmony and stability, and to strengthen the CPC's leading and governing capabilities. Fourthly, marked by the Decisions of the Central Committee of the Communist Party of China on Some Major Issues Concerning Comprehensively Deepening the Reform, the CPC has formed a systemic top-level design plan for all-round and further reform, ushering in a new era of reforms in China's economy, politics, culture, society, ecology, and Party building.

Achievement two: reform of the economic system taking the lead

The central role of economic reform determines that the economic system must take the lead. Since CPC held its 18th National Congress in 2012, a clear plan has been developed in this regard. By clarifying the decisive role of the market in resource allocation, we will be able to improve the market system, stop excessive government intervention, strengthen government supervision, break the growth bottleneck for the next decade, and counter the potential downward pressure on growth. By further improving the management of state assets, we will be able to put capital management in a prominent position and strengthen supervision of state assets. By establishing a budget management system, we will be able to improve the tax system and the system to adapt the authority of office to expenditure responsibility, improve resource allocation, ensure unified markets, promote social fairness, and maintain long-term stability. By orderly promoting of mixed ownership reform and other forms of reform, we will be able to overcome institutional flaws and boost business vitality.

Achievements in economic reform have brought about changes in other sectors. Politically, efforts have been strengthened to reform government institutions and transform government functions. Several ministerial-level offices have been canceled and the power of administrative examination and approval for a plethora of matters has been delegated to lower levels. Reform on such scale and at such a level has never been seen before. Socially, a series of innovative reform measures have been proposed for systemic and institutional improvement. Under a new agricultural business system, farmers have been granted more property rights, and resources and services are now flowing between urban and rural areas unimpeded. On the legal front, goals of implementing the socialist rule of law have been announced, and reforms in the judiciary have begun to build a complete system of legal norms, an efficient system of law enforcement, a strict system of legal oversight, a forceful system of legal guarantee, and a sound system of intra-Party laws and regulations. Reforms in the cultural and ecological sectors are also picking up momentum, and major breakthroughs have been made in national defense and military reforms.

Achievement three: reform benefits being distributed in an orderly fashion

Through comprehensive reform in focal areas, systemic and institutional innovation has released both visible and invisible benefits. First, people's minds have been opened so that further reforms are made possible. Through these reforms, the entire nation will gain a deeper understanding of its importance, and realize that reform is the only choice China has, that supporting the reform means supporting development and embracing the future. With the release of reform benefits, facts have proven that the reform so far has been effective and productive, that a sound environment conducive to promoting reform has been formed, and that reformers have gained the respect and support they deserve. Second, a series of policies have been enacted in support of reform plans. Focusing on the overall objective of all-round and further reform, supporting policies and measures have been announced in different areas. Guiding documents on the reform of state-owned enterprises and military reform have garnered strong support from the society, and further enhanced the implementation of overall reform. Third, by streamlining administration and delegating powers to lower levels, the government is able to give more freedom to businesses, which will have more autonomy over their management. In this way, businesses are showing vitality while governments improve efficiency and functions. Fourth, the reforms in ensuring people's well-being have brought actual benefits to ordinary people, who are gaining more benefits and living happier lives.

IV. Combating Corruption, the Rule of Law, and New Political Ecology

Achievements

- Improving conduct by implementing Party discipline
- Zero tolerance of corruption and a tougher stance on combating corruption
- Establishing the rule of law in all areas

Long-term governance is prone to corruption. Without action, it will only lead to the downfall of the CPC and the collapse of the state. To continue to govern, the CPC must be resolute in eradicating corruption, promoting clean governance, and ensuring social fairness and justice, in order to win the trust of the people. Following its 18th National Congress, the CPC leadership, cutting in from strengthening Party conduct, has fought a war against the "four forms of decadence" (formalism, bureaucratism, hedonism and extravagance). It has carried out rigorous campaigns against corruption and upholding Party discipline, decisively strengthening the rule of law and promoting justice. Focusing on Party conduct and the fight against corruption, the leadership has taken the initiative to thoroughly implement Party discipline and the rule of law, and to build a new political ecology in contemporary China.

Achievement one: improving conduct by implementing Party discipline

Ensuring cohesiveness in the Party relies not only on conviction, but also on discipline. To run the Party with strict discipline, Party regulations must be thoroughly implemented and violations of Party discipline must be dealt with resolutely. Only in this way can Party conduct be truly improved. At a political bureau meeting of the CPC Committee following CPC's 18th National Congress, Xi Jinping chaired the session and approved the "eight regulations" on improving conduct and maintaining close ties with the people. By launching an education program on the Party's principle of staying in close touch with the people and the fight against the "four forms of decadence" within CPC's rank and file, the leadership quickly made clear its stance against bad conduct and corruption. By focusing on the key problems, the campaign has helped CPC members and officials realize their problems and examine their conduct, to allow a deeper understanding of the hazards of the "four forms of decadence" and press them to improve their conduct. To bring Party regulations up to date to address current problems, the CPC has amended the Regulations of the Communist Party of China on Disciplinary Actions, and the Code of Conduct on Integrity and Discipline for Members of the Communist Party of China, making a "negative list" of problems of Party organizations and members in executing Party discipline in politics, organization, integrity, mass relations, work, and life. In the past few years, solid progress has been made in implementing strict Party discipline and in punishing any violation of the rules. In 2014 and in January to October of 2015, a total of 80,000 violations of the "eight regulations" were investigated and 100,000 persons were punished. Among the 50,000 people who received disciplinary punishments, seven were ministerial-level officials. All these efforts have contributed to the authority of the Party's discipline and regulations, strengthened Party members' reverence for the institutions, enhanced their awareness of self-discipline, and improved Party conduct, clean governance, and social ethos.

Achievement two: zero tolerance of corruption and a tougher stance on combating corruption

Bad conduct leads to corruption. While maintaining a resolute stance against the "four forms of decadence," the new generation of the CPC leadership has zero tolerance for corruption, and strives to deal with the two at the same time. In the fight against corruption, there is no forbidden zone, no blind spot, no exception, and no end to eliminating the evil. The campaign targets both "tigers" and "flies," and corrupt officials in China and hiding overseas, exposing and punishing corrupt officials at all levels from those accepting large bribes in the high ranks to lower-level officials who undermine the immediate interests of the people. The new round of the anti-corruption campaign is highlighted by the following traits: One, the CPC must abide by laws and regulations, ensuring equality before the law for suspects, and setting no cap or limit on the ranks of officials investigated. Two, effort must focus on those who have not shown constraint after the 18th CPC National Congress held in 2012, those who are already the targets of investigation with supporting evidence, those who have been reported for misconduct, and those who are holding important offices and might be promoted. Three, the campaign must be expanded to the discipline inspection team. The fight against corruption not only targets officials at all levels, but also at the discipline inspection team itself. Over the past few years, a group of high-ranking officials, including Zhou Yongkang, Guo Boxiong, Xu Caihou, Ling Jihua, and Su Rong, have been investigated and prosecuted for corruption, and the number of investigated officials above the vice-ministerial level more than doubled compared to five years ago. At the Commission for Discipline Inspection of the CPC Central Committee, misconduct was also investigated, resulting in the arrest of Wei Jian, head of the Fourth Discipline Inspection Office. The number of officials investigated and the intensity of the campaign had never been seen before. These efforts have won the trust of the Party and people. Chinese people have made such comments: "The Party Central Committee has pulled out 'malignant tumors' and cut out sloughs; our Party has begun to restore vitality." "The cancer of corruption used to be fatal, but now we do not doubt our Party's ability to regenerate." "China has hope; the people have hope; and socialism has hope!" Facts have proven that the anti-corruption fight, with wide support from the people, has improved the CPC's image and increased government credibility. The fight against corruption will not affect the economy. On the contrary, it will create a better environment for economic development in China by bringing more confidence and strength to the CPC.

Achievement three: establishing the rule of law by abolishing obsolete laws and enacting new laws

Running the Party with discipline is the basis of implementing the rule of law in China, and the rule of law in turn ensures the implementation of Party discipline. CPC's 18th National Congress initiated discipline- and law-based Party and national governance. Firstly, the CPC sought to improve the system of laws and regulations by abolishing obsolete laws and enacting new ones. Party regulations underwent a complete overhaul, the first of its kind since 1978, abolishing 40 percent of the regulations and guiding documents that were no longer applicable to modern times. In the meantime, the legislature has been strengthened to reflect the new trends in socioeconomic development, with the announcement of the Regulations on the Formulation of Intra-Party Regulations of the Communist Party of China and Regulations on Practicing Stringency and Combating Waste at Party and Government Offices. Major amendments have been made to laws regarding the punishment for corruption, and the standard regarding conviction and punishment for bribery has been made clear. Moreover, top-level design has been strengthened to implement the rule of law. In the Decisions of the CPC Central Committee on Some Major Issues Regarding Thoroughly Implementing the Rule of Law, the CPC set forth the goals of building China's socialist rule of law, and raising the rule of law to a higher level for orderly implementation. Secondly, the CPC sought to ensure the core value of fairness and justice by setting models and correcting mistakes. More efforts have been made in strengthening theoretical and institutional innovation to ensure fairness and justice. By establishing circuit courts and cross-regional people's courts and people's prosecuting bodies, the people's courts and people's prosecutors have been able to rule out interference in judicial and prosecution procedures, ensuring that the courts and prosecutors exercise their powers consistent with the law independently and impartially. Efforts have also been made to uphold justice, and a number of unjust, false and misjudged cases, such as the cases of Huge Jiletu and Nian Bin, have been corrected based on the facts. The sanctity of the law has been protected, and the rule of law has never been so genuinely felt.

For its resolve and achievements in combating corruption and implementing the rule of law, the CPC's new generation of central leadership has won wide acclaim and support from the people and inspired self-discipline among the officials. As the campaign has been carried out across the nation, the use of power has been put under institutional checks and made more transparent, promoting good conduct and uprightness. It is increasingly evident that in modern China, people have more opportunities and channels to develop, "unspoken rules" have lost their magic, and fairness and justice have become a central theme.

V. Thoroughly Implementing Party Discipline

Achievements
- Running the Party with strict discipline
- Innovating the institutions to govern officials
- Cultivating confidence and conviction in the cause

During the long process of China's revolution–its nation-building, reform, opening up, and understanding the current stage of development—Party building has always been a secret to success. As reform is driven to deeper levels and China opens up more, the CPC is faced with unprecedented risks and challenges. It must improve Party building, and run the Party with strict discipline. Since the CPC's 18th National Congress, the new generation of CPC leadership holds onto Party building as a key project in the new stage of development, faithfully performing the duties of governing and running the Party with strict discipline. It has achieved many positive results in improving the Party's governing capacity, maintaining the CPC's advanced nature and purity, and innovating Party building in all respects. The positive tradition has been reestablished to boost CPC's confidence, improve its image, and consolidate its status.

Achievement one: restoring the positive tradition of running the Party with strict discipline

Abandoning tradition and forgetting one's roots will sever one from one's cultural heritage. To address slackened Party building and boost Party image, the CPC's new leadership has made timely analyses of the root causes in search of solutions. First of all, it has focused on strictly running the Party as specified in the Party constitution and regulations. With the Party constitution as a guidebook of conduct, Party members have once again taken the initiative to abide by the constitution, implementing it and safeguarding its authority. Secondly, it has passed down the revolutionary tradition and strengthening education on conviction and commitment. Party members are required to dig into the origin of their belief, replenish the "marrow" of their convictions, and pass down the positive traditions of Party building and improve themselves on its basis. In this way, problems and crises in relation to beliefs and conviction can be curbed. Thirdly, it has focused on Party building in grassroots organizations. Party committees at grassroots levels have played a large role in consolidating Party building at lower levels, so that a solid foundation can be laid to complete the mission.

Achievement two: governing the Party and officials through institutional innovation

To run the Party with strict discipline, the key lies in setting up rules and institutions. Since 2012, the CPC has put a large amount of effort into innovating the institutions of Party governance, adopting a series of measures that ensure Party members perform their duties and uphold political integrity. Firstly, political discipline and rules have been reaffirmed. Elevating political discipline and rules to a paramount position among all

Party regulations has further enhanced the political nature of Party building. Secondly, oversight of Party officials has been improved. Inspection tours have played a key role in running and reinforcing the Party's strict discipline and discovering existing problems. With strengthened and innovated efforts, inspection tours have been effective in deterring misconduct and corruption. Officials are required to report relevant personal matters to the Party, and the examination and accountability mechanism has been strengthened to supervise and admonish Party officials. Thirdly, the key responsibilities of the Party committees have been thoroughly implemented. It has been made clear that failure of Party committees to carry out Party building is a dereliction of duty, and incompetence in carrying out Party building results in malfeasance. By prioritizing Party building and clarifying the responsibilities of Party committees at different levels, the key responsibility of Party committees in promoting Party building has been clearly defined. By reforming the discipline inspection system and improving the anti-corruption mechanism, power has been checked and oversight has been strengthened, ensuring that the supervisory function of discipline inspection committees is operated independently.

Achievement three: cultivating confidence and conviction in the cause

Confidence is in the nature of Chinese Communists. The courage to self-purify, self-improve, and self-innovate is what enables the CPC to lead the nation. In recent years, the new generation of CPC leadership, by focusing on the problems, combating corruption and the "four forms of decadence," and setting good examples by themselves, has carried out targeted measures to strengthen Party discipline and improve Party conduct. Deep-rooted problems undermining stability have been addressed one-by-one, lost traditions have been recovered, and the Party has once again been rejuvenated and the conviction in the cause reaffirmed. The CPC will stand in the center of the historical stage and at the front of the times, to lead the Chinese people in the great cause from victory to victory.

Running the Party with strict discipline has effectively improved the political ecology inside the CPC, banishing unhealthy tendencies and bad influences. It has also enabled the CPC to purify itself through an internal mechanism, and significantly strengthened intra-Party cohesiveness, the people's trust, social credibility, and international influence.

VI. Diplomacy and a New World Order

Achievements
- Abandoning a zero-sum mentality for wiser diplomacy
- Safeguarding national sovereignty and holding onto the baseline of diplomatic principles
- Cooperation, mutual benefit, development, and open diplomacy

National rejuvenation calls for successful diplomacy. In this time of great change, China needs to develop its diplomacy to suit its status. Since the new generation of the CPC leadership took office, it put developing a new diplomatic strategy in a prominent position in governance, carrying forward the positive tradition of Chinese diplomacy and creating a new pattern of diplomacy in line with the current stage of development and its goals. The practice has proven fruitful in the handling of international relations, in improving China's global image, safeguarding world peace, and building a new world order.

Achievement one: abandoning the zero-sum mentality for wiser diplomacy

On the basis of peaceful development, the CPC leadership

has bravely abandoned the zero-sum mentality, and cultivated a new image of being pragmatic, confident, and inclusive. In handling China's relations with other countries, the leadership makes sure that equality and balance are prioritized, being resolute on the rightful claims and reasonable on other concerns. Today, China is carrying out its multifaceted global diplomacy in these areas: improving relations with Russia, reinforcing trade relations with the EU and other important European countries, making progress with the US in building a new relationship between major countries, strengthening cooperation with developing countries, especially in Africa, and deepening relations with countries in Latin America. Based in the Asia Pacific region, China has been reaching out to countries around the globe in its pursuit of a new global strategy.

Achievement two: safeguarding national sovereignty and holding onto the baseline of diplomatic principles

Since 2012, the new leadership, upholding national sovereignty as the paramount principle, has strictly followed international common practices, exercised flexibility in the use of diplomatic strategies, and actively mobilized diplomatic resources, to safeguard national sovereignty and development interests. While sticking to peaceful development, China has also kept to its standards of never giving up its rightful interests and never sacrificing core national interests. It held onto this standard when dealing with the territorial disputes with Japan, the Philippines, Vietnam, and India, resolutely countering any foreign attempt to threaten its territorial integrity. With an active strategy, China showed the world its principles and baseline on core interests.

Achievement three: cooperation, mutual benefit, development, and open diplomacy

For the first time, cooperation and mutual benefit became a banner of Chinese diplomacy, which features equality and mutual trust, cooperation and mutual benefit, exchanges and mutual learning, mutual support and help, and unity and collaboration, and is based on joint consultation, joint construction, and sharing of benefits. The pragmatic guidelines contributed to the development of China's open diplomacy—to begin with, taking the initiative to show good faith. In the past few years, President Xi traveled around the globe to make friends, delineating a new diplomatic roadmap and creating many "firsts" in the history of Chinese diplomacy. He also developed new methods of promoting mutual benefit overseas. By proposing the building of the Silk Road Economic Belt and the 21st century Maritime Silk Road, known as the B&R Initiative, China has laid the foundation for interconnectivity and cooperation with Central Asia and ASEAN nations. By founding the Asian Infrastructure Investment Bank, China is able to integrate into international finance. These strategies and measures have made it possible for the global economy to integrate and develop, providing China with a firm platform from which to practice its diplomacy of reciprocity and further participate in global governance. Over the past few years, Xi Jinping has shown confidence and openness on the international stage, giving a voice to China's philosophies and providing solutions to the world's problems in an effort to promote cooperation on a larger scale and at higher levels. China's role is being redefined on the international stage. With its voice heard, China is becoming an increasingly important player in global governance with its active attitude and awareness of its responsibilities.

There is no doubt that Chinese diplomacy in the last few years has attracted wide attention in international politics. With vision, courage, wisdom and strength, President Xi has opened a new era of Chinese diplomacy.

To sum up, since taking charge of the Party, government and

military, President Xi has pushed a series of new measures in governance, bringing about huge changes to the country, instilling vitality to the Party and society, distributing benefits to the people, and making the Chinese a more proud and happy people. Implementing a new round of overall reform, carrying forward the fight against corruption, upgrading the economic structure, and promoting global diplomacy, China is gaining momentum towards common prosperity. With one heart, the CPC and the people are working hard to carry forward China's socialist cause, and breaking new ground for realizing the Chinese Dream. China's future is promising; it will become a country of great international influence.

CHAPTER TWO

Interpreting Xi Jinping's Governance Philosophies

Key Phrases

In his practice of governance over the past few years, Xi Jinping has implemented the following four strategies:

- Steering the direction of future development
- Leading national development with modern thinking
- Igniting an internal driving force of reform and innovation
- Mustering strength from all walks of life for national rejuvenation

In practicing governance, Xi Jinping has showcased his grand vision, strategic thinking, originality, and intense, careful planning. It's inspiring to see that Xi's success in governance is a result of his accurate understanding of core issues and his performance of "political convictions, scientific governance, reform and innovation, and people-oriented planning." Based on his governance, Xi has concentrated his efforts in four areas with noticeable progress.

I. Steering the Direction of Future Development

Strategies

- Cultivating political convictions in the correct direction
- Governing officials with strict discipline
- Building a strong army
- Working toward realizing the Chinese Dream

After three decades of development, China has completed its first half of modernization, and now it is embarking on a new journey of modernizing its national governance system and capabilities. Based on the accomplishments made from high-speed growth, China must continue to progress in this new historical stage. To do this, it must stay on the right course and maintain control of the overall situation, properly handle existing problems while dealing with new problems, and address emergencies in a timely manner. At a time of leadership transition, the complexity of intertwining domestic and international issues and the difficult problems of interests and position-taking are prone to affect people's mindset and values, and might lead to erroneous judgment of the political scene. People with ulterior motives will not let this chance of meddling in China's affairs go.

In fact, not long after CPC's 18th National Congress in 2012, some began to question the future and path of China's development and its system. There were open criticisms of the government, as well as some "elixirs for all ills" and "reform plans" offered to China. Hostile forces in the West also took the opportunity to sell their type of "universal values" and Western systems through agents, with the intention to manipulate China's direction and shake the base of the CPC. With political acumen and insight, Xi Jinping met these challenges head on and without hesitation, while taking resolute action to answer the questions regarding China's future and path in the new era.

These answers have lifted the mist shrouding China's development, eliminated ideological obstacles, cleared the way for governance, and expanded the channels for future development, creating favorable conditions for winning this new historic battle.

Strategy one: cultivating political convictions in the correct direction

The path determines fate, and direction determines the future. For Xi, what kind of road to take is the fundamental question in relation to the survival of the CPC and the nation, and the success of the socialist cause. As soon as he took office, he admonished the entire CPC, "China is a large country. We cannot afford to make disastrous mistakes on fundamental problems," which showed a high level of political conviction.

First, he needed strong political convictions in the fundamental question of "banner and path." As pointed out by Xi, socialism with Chinese characteristics is the banner of unity, progress, and victory of the CPC and the Chinese people; it marks the direction of development and progress in contemporary China. Advancing on the path of Chinese socialism will lead to the realization of the socialist ideal, and the action should be guided by the theoretical system and guaranteed by all institutions—all integral components of the great practice of socialism in China. By summarizing the 500 years of experience and lessons of world efforts for socialism, Xi told the CPC that at any time, Party members should maintain confidence in our paths, theories, system and culture of the country, and that every Chinese person should be confident in our ultimate success. He said, "Only the wearer knows whether his shoes suit him, and only the people of a country know whether their path of development suits their nation," which vividly explained why the Chinese under CPC leadership had chosen the path of socialism. He also said, "We respect the rights of the people of the world to independently choose their paths of development, and we stand against intervention in the internal affairs of other countries, and strive to safeguard international fairness and justice." These remarks demonstrate that the path of socialism, a choice of the Chinese people, has deep roots in history, in practice, and in the public. China will never allow anyone to undermine this path, because it is the result of its historical choices, of the call of the times, and of the aspirations of its people. The Chinese will be more confident in winning the ultimate victory and in developing socialism with vigor and enthusiasm.

Second, he needed strong political conviction in the question of leadership by the CPC. According to Xi, the leadership of the CPC is the fundamental characteristic of Chinese socialism, and the guarantee for the socialist rule of law. The central task of running the Party with strict discipline lies in strengthening Party leadership. Xi pointed out that as long as the Party is strong, as long as the Party maintains close ties with the people, the country will prosper and maintain stability, and the people will lead happy lives. He also stressed that the absolute leadership of the CPC over the army must never be challenged. Under the guidance of these rules, Xi Jinping has made CPC leadership the core and lifeline of the Party and nation, which is closely related to the interests of the people. In the Four-Pronged Strategy, implementing Party discipline ensures that reform in the other three aspects is carried out. The ultimate goal of doing so is to strengthen Party leadership with a theoretical and institutional foundation so that, under the leadership of the CPC, the Chinese Dream will be achieved, reform will be brought to profound levels, the growth model will be transformed, and the rule of law will be fully implemented.

Third, he needed strong conviction in struggles for political guidance. Under the present circumstances, China faces an unprecedented level of ideological struggle and complexity. On the one hand, hostile Western forces are trying hard to sell their systems and values, and challenging our governing base by disseminating ideas of neoliberalism, democratic socialism, and historical nihilism. On the other, individuals with ulterior motives are tarnishing the image of our leaders and national heroes in denial of history, by brewing and spreading rumors, and slandering the state apparatus and SOEs. Aggravated by certain issues concerning people's lives, the shock of social transformation on core values coupled with negative information on the Internet, certain segments of the public have been misled and different voices permeated society to challenge the people's values. In response, Xi Jinping resolutely struggled to make political guidance an important fuction of the CPC, emphasizing that the Party must firmly hold onto the rights of leadership, governance, and speech, showing great political convictions undeterred by any form of disruption. On matters of principle, he took the initiative to address pressing problems with great political courage, and has asked the entire Party to guard the "red zone," restrict the "black zone," and transform the "gray zone" regarding public opinions. In the struggle against inaccurate mindsets, Xi maintained a clear head and calmly dealt with the challenges, emphasizing the main theme and positive energy, especially when dealing with key issues such as the basic system of socialism. His response has been firm and resolute, and has never backed off or left any room for imagination.

Xi Jinping's resolve on matters of direction and importance dealt heavy blows to the hostile forces seeking to overthrow socialism in China. The entire CPC has strengthened the convictions of Party leadership and the Chinese path of socialism; it has been firmly united toward the future and the Chinese Dream.

Strategy two: governing officials with strict discipline

To govern the country, the CPC must first be governed; to govern the CPC, the officials must first be governed. Once the political platform is set, officials become the decisive factor.

Facts have proven that no fatal problem will arise as long as the officials perform their duties. As the Two Centenary Goals are set and with the proposal of the Chinese Dream, the CPC, its members and officials have been required to improve their performance by setting higher standards. Following CPC's 18th National Congress, Xi Jinping established the goal of strengthening the team building of officials by introducing a series of new thoughts about governing officials with strict discipline. In detail, these include strengthening supervision over top officials in line with the conditions of the Party and country, upholding innovation in the governance system and organization, and the planning and coordination for officials to develop in all aspects. By innovating the system and acquiring experience, team building of officials is steadily improving, laying a solid organizational basis for the CPC's management of state affairs.

First, clear standards are needed on the selection of officials. To build a capable team of officials, standards must come in first, and the standards for good performance should be objective, current, easy to measure, and recognized by all. For a long period of time, the standards for a good official had been vague and hard to quantify, restricting the development of China's officials. Learning from his past experience when he served as the head of local CPC committees and when he oversaw the organizational work at the Central Committee, Xi Jinping proposed the standards of good officials in the new era: Firm conviction, serving the people, diligence and pragmatism, the courage to take on responsibilities, and integrity and clean governance. These standards created the model and direction for all Chinese officials. Further efforts were made to enrich the contents of these standards. When meeting with the secretaries of local CPC committees who were studying in Beijing, Xi asked them to "hold the Party, the people, their responsibilities, and discipline to heart." When meeting with CPC committee secretaries with outstanding performance, Xi encouraged them to "have clear political principles, lead the way in development, understand the peo-

ple's needs, and exercise good leadership in CPC committees."
At the national conference of CPC schools, he further asked
Party officials to "forge will as iron-like belief, conviction, discipline, and commitment." All these requirements have offered
clear guidance on the direction and standards of team-building
for Party officials, and detailed requirements have been made
for different positions, offices, levels, and sectors in light of local conditions. The standards have thus been enriched and improved. With these standards, CPC organizations are now clear
about the direction for training and promoting officials, officials
themselves have tangible goals, and the public knows what to
expect from officials. Ideals, actions, responsibilities, and vener-
ation have become the new scale for Chinese officials.

Second, new thinking is needed in the selection of officials.
On the basis of clarified standards, Xi Jinping made a timely
adjustment of the focus on innovating the system for the management of officials, to ensure that the CPC manages its officials, boosts their vitality, and selects outstanding officials to
serve the Party and the people. To strengthen the role of CPC
organizations in the selection and promotion of officials, CPC
committees now have a larger say in the process, and organizational departments are required to take more responsibility in
examining and selecting officials. Instead of just counting the
votes, CPC organizations should strengthen Party leadership
and exercise democracy in these procedures. To reinvigorate
the selection process, improve the credibility of recommen-
dations and examinations, and counter Western influences in
the methods of selection, a new set of criteria has been set to
effectively and efficiently select capable officials. The examination and selection processes have been strengthened based on
the five standards of good performance, to ensure that officials
who are firm in their beliefs, outstanding in their work, good
in conduct, and popular with the people be selected. To reduce
overdependence on votes, exam results, and technical index-
es, the CPC has innovated the principles for selecting officials,

and stopped considering only such factors as votes, exam grades, GDP readings, and age. To examine candidates with a comprehensive approach, organizational departments are required to make contact with officials through different channels and from different sources, to go to the places where they work and the people they work with, and to make comprehensive evaluation of their knowledge, qualities, abilities, performance, and ways of dealing with emergencies, so that candidates are appraised with objectivity, impartiality, and credibility. To improve age-related criteria, so that both young and capable officials and older and more experienced officials have equal opportunities to succeed, so that personnel resources are fully utilized.

Third, strict management of officials is needed. Strict management of officials is an important tool to ensure the correct political direction and effectiveness of the officials. Since assuming the leading position of the CPC in late 2012, Xi Jinping has escalated strict management of officials to a prominent position, setting strict requirements for the management and discipline of Party officials. CPC officials must safeguard the authority of the Central Committee, must maintain unity and cohesiveness of the Party, must abide by organizational procedures, must comply with the decisions of the Party, and must discipline their relatives and staff. With the implementation of the "eight regulations" and the education program on the Party's principle of maintaining close touch with the people, CPC is continuing its effort to combat the "four forms of decadence" and practice the "the three guidelines for ethical behavior and the three basic rules of conduct (the 3+3 Initiative)." Setting good examples for lower levels, CPC leadership has pushed the campaign to deeper levels and made it a regular task. To address such issues as promoting problematic officials, failure to perform one's duties of office, and lax implementation of discipline, the CPC has issued targeted regulations, such as the Regulations on the Promotion and Demotion of Officials, to improve the management of officials, and ensure the purity and good performance of the team. Meanwhile, the supervision of lower-level CPC organizations by higher levels has been strengthened with concrete progress in investigating acts of violation by officials, in examining the reporting of relevant personal matters, and in regulating concurrent office in violation of the rules. All these have contributed to increased reverence for Party discipline and the sound management of officials.

By governing officials with strict discipline, the CPC is able to hold onto the "key minority," and make rectification from the root, effectively strengthening the management of officials. In addition to setting the standards of selecting officials and creating a sound political ecology, it has also helped officials enhance their abilities of self-purification, self-improvement, and self-innovation, laying the basis for personal integrity, a clean government, and upright politics, and offering valuable support to the path of Chinese socialism and to the grand future of the Chinese Dream.

Strategy three: building a strong army

The people's army and armed police forces are the cornerstone of China. They shoulder the sacred responsibilities of safeguarding the country, people's well-being, peace and stability, and the historical mission of guarding the reform and opening up drive. Carrying forward the reform, promoting the transformation of the growth model, developing democratic politics, and realizing CPC's self-innovation cannot be done without a stable political environment, harmonious social environment, and a peaceful international environment. Building a strong army in service of the country is a responsibility placed on the army by the CPC and the country. As chairman of the Central Military Commission, Xi Jinping has, in the last few years, brought military preparedness to a prominent position, vigorously promoting political and military progress and pushing reforms in the army, bringing about great changes.

First, it was critical to support the army with political conviction. It is determined by the nature of people's army that politics must be placed above all else. Only an army with strong conviction can win battles and wars, and can be trusted in times of crisis. Following CPC's 18th National Congress, Xi Jinping, with a deep understanding of the pressing problems in army building and based on the need for long-lasting stability, has taken the initiative to strengthen the army's conviction in its mission and invoke the pride in its tradition. Absolute leadership of the CPC over the army has been reinforced, in that the people's army must always follow the orders of the Party, be loyal to the Party, and be of one heart with the Party. The army must always follow the orders of the Party Central Committee, safeguard its authority, and always be the loyal guardians of the Party and the people. Good traditions should never be discarded. One tradition of the army is its theoretical and political work, which is being strengthened with the opening of the army's conference on political work. In accordance with Xi Jinping's requirements to firmly establish conviction in the mission, political integrity and principles, standards of combat effectiveness, and authority of political work, four core aspects in strengthening the army, the people's army is thoroughly implementing the key tasks of building the army with political conviction. The strength in theoretical work has been maintained and passed down. The people's army must be built with strong political and theoretical bases. In a peaceful environment, it is inevitable that problems will arise in terms of conviction, integrity and principles, the revolutionary spirit, and discipline and conduct. This is why consolidating the army's beliefs and cultivating a new generation of soldiers that are combat-ready and have personal integrity is a vital task. In the meantime, the army must be strictly run; its lingering illnesses must be cured, and any misconduct that affects CPC leadership must be corrected. Efforts must also be made in strengthening belief and conviction, in fighting the pessimistic attitude towards war preparedness and against reform, in untangling interest networks, in tackling cronyism and nepotism, in eradicating bad conduct, and in reestablishing the political image and authority of the army. Resolute actions have been taken in order to investigate and punish corrupt officers, including Guo Boxiong, Xu Caihou, and Gu Junshan, to cleanse the army and ensure stability. Through these efforts, the army has welcomed healthy development with renewed conviction.

Second, it was important to strengthen the army with military preparedness. Modern warfare has undergone profound changes. China's army has not fought in any war for many years, and its composition has also changed. To ensure military preparedness and increase combat effectiveness, Xi Jinping has initiated a new campaign to build a strong army under absolute CPC leadership. A peaceful environment is prone to giving rise to laxity and fear of war in the army. It is a proven fact that only with military preparedness can a nation prevent war. The army exists to fight; this nature will not change as time changes. After he took over the Military Commission of the CPC Central Committee, Xi has made sure that the army is combat ready at any time. The entire army must take combat readiness as the top priority; soldiers must be able to fight, officers must be able to command the army towards victory, and the entire army must always be ready to fight in battles. By strengthening military preparedness over the past few years, marked improvement has been made in the army's combat readiness and war preparedness. Efforts have also been made in strengthening the army's combat capability, through intensified training and careful preparation. Xi Jinping believes that the army must be prepared to fight in real wars, which requires the implementation of top-level training and use of authentic settings. Training methods have been innovated to strengthen competitive training and drills with live ammunition, to simulate real war conditions. CPC committees and officers at all levels of the military must focus their efforts on war preparedness and implement the strategies of the Central Committee. For a few years the entire army has been striving to enhance combat effectiveness as a main theme of their work, examining and evaluating military performance with this criterion, so that combat effectiveness will always be a key measurement of military development. Another area that has seen progress is the level of armament. In modern warfare, advanced arms are playing an increasingly important role. Victory is only possible by fully integrating the factors of man and equipment. With deep insights, Xi put the advancement of weaponry on the agenda, closely followed the latest development in military technology, and planned for the development of high-technology equipment, consolidating the technical basis for modernizing national defense and the army. All these efforts have led to marked progress in China's military strength, as evident in the military parade commemorating the 70th anniversary of the Chinese People's War of Resistance Against Japanese Aggression and the World Anti-Fascist War in 2015. The weapons and arms shown in the parade reached international advanced levels, with 84 percent making their debut. The two models of anti-ship ballistic missiles, the first in the world, awed the world and made the Chinese people proud.

Third, strengthening the army through reform became a priority. Around the world major powers are reforming their armies in pursuit of military advantages. Xi Jinping has keenly noticed that in this new military revolution, those who refuse to make progress will miss the opportunity and suffer a strategic disadvantage. China must grab the chance and take action. To improve the level of military management, develop a joint operational command system, rearrange the army's structure, and reform backward areas, Xi has included national defense and military reform in the planning of further reform. He has made the mission a priority of the CPC and the nation, and brought the most profound changes in the army in the history of the PRC. For its new contents in terms of top-level design, organization and implementation, risk control, and actual effects, military reforms set a milestone in building the people's army, and will certainly exert long-lasting influence over army building. The reform featured many "firsts," solved a variety of problems, made a series of breakthroughs, and positively affected other areas. First of all, the reform was carefully planned at the top level. A new pattern has been established with the Central Military Commission overseeing overall work, military commands in charge of war preparedness, and different services building their own teams, as well as an operational command system of "commission-command-army" and a management hierarchy of "commission-service-army." Second, the reform had clear targets. It closely focused on modernizing the army and improving the ability to fight computer-based warfare, addressing the ultimate goal of military reform. Third, the reform was intended to solve problems. With furthering reform and eradicating chronic ills in mind, the reform pinpointed the root causes for the problems, and broke the bottleneck restricting army building. Lastly, the reform was closely connected to reforms in other areas. National defense and army building have been integrated in the economic and social system on a larger scale and at a higher level, underlined by efficient, multiple factors and all-sector integration.

Army building by promoting conviction, combat readiness, and further reform will bring about revolutionary changes in the Chinese army, which will see overall improvement. In the future, China's army will grow stronger and more vigorous, and will provide powerful support to guarding the country and realizing the Chinese Dream.

Strategy four: working towards realizing the Chinese Dream

A nation will only have hope when it has dreams; a political party will have a bright future only when it aspires to achieve. As China opens up to the rest of the world, its economy grows rapidly, productive forces constantly improve, and the people lead richer lives. It is true that as decadent and negative thinking began to brew, self-interest is hollowing out belief and conviction, tainting people's conduct, and injecting utilitarian thoughts into society. This unhealthy trend is undoubtedly putting at risk the ultimate goal of the CPC and its national rejuvenation strategy. To reach a consensus inside and outside the Party and muster all strength for reviving the people's ideals, shortly after CPC's 18th National Congress, Xi Jinping made a timely proposition of the Chinese Dream, leading the Chinese people to achieve the grand goal.

First, he built consensus and set the direction. The proposition of the Chinese Dream gives voice to the aspiration of the CPC, and how to let the people understand and relate to the Chinese Dream will directly affect China's future direction and the realization of the dream. After CPC's 18th National Congress, Xi Jinping offered a systemic explanation of its contents and significance, crystallizing the goals and tasks of the CPC and the country into the Chinese Dream. With the proposal of the Four-Pronged Comprehensives and Five-in-One Development philosophies, the Chinese Dream is becoming enriched and more tangible. It is inspiring the Chinese nation with aspirations and hope.

Second, he found the root in the people. Only by taking root in the people will the Chinese Dream come true. "The Chinese Dream, in the final analysis, is the dream of the people, and relies on the people to realize," says Xi. It is the dream of the country, of the nation, and of the people. The Chinese Dream is not an empty shell, nor a slogan, but a tangible and specific goal, affecting the immediate interests of every Chinese. It not only influences their lives, but also guides their work and pursuit of personal goals. Shared by all, the Chinese Dream has the greatest number of beneficiaries whose common interests are the rejuvenation of the Chinese nation.

Third, he chose the right path. The Chinese Dream is being treated by some as a simple concept or misinterpreted as lopsided or material. To address the misunderstanding, Xi Jinping explained the path to realize the Chinese Dream, correcting misinterpretations and showing the right path. To begin with, the principle is that in realizing the Chinese Dream, we must take our own path, pool our strengths together, and hold on to peaceful development. Next, the steps are to complete the building of a moderately prosperous society in all respects by the time the CPC celebrates its centennial in 2021, and complete the building of a modern socialist country by the time the PRC celebrates its centennial in 2049. These steps have made the grand goals of the Chinese Dream more tangible. Finally, the path to realize the Chinese Dream lies in our daily work, in our continuing efforts, and in our firm conviction. Also, in realizing the Chinese Dream, we must integrate with the world and maintain inclusiveness.

"With wind beneath my wings, I soar to the sky." The proposition of the Chinese Dream has been received with warm responses by the Chinese, who are united under one goal to obtain a better future for the country.

Standing on this important juncture, Xi Jinping is calmly and boldly upholding the banner of Chinese socialism, strictly implementing discipline in the Party, among officials, and in the army. Pushing forward the reform to deeper levels, thoroughly implementing the rule of law, and building a firm base of governance, Xi is proudly leading the people towards the rejuvenation of the Chinese nation.

II. Leading National Development with Modern Thinking

Strategies

- Top-level design for modern governance system
- Higher level of governing capabilities
- Practicing governance through multiple channels

- The art of governance and techniques

National governance has a vital bearing on a country's economic, political, cultural, social, and ecological development. Summarizing the successes and failures of China and other socialist nations, Xi Jinping realized that to sustain healthy development, the governance system and governing capabilities must be constantly improved. This is why after he took charge of the overall work of the CPC, state, and military, Xi, a visionary statesman and strategist, transformed national administration to governance, put the big question of how to govern a socialist country in front of the entire Party, and was determined to find a path different than capitalist roads and one that suits China. Keenly aware of the key issues in relation to the long-lasting governance of the CPC and the development of the country, Xi put forward a top-level design with vision and wisdom, broke barriers with courage, and quickly initiated a campaign to enhance governance capabilities. This will play a key part in driving modernization in China.

Strategy one: top-level design for modern governance system

The national governance system is a closely-knit mechanism of coordination at the national level. Sound top-level design ensures the functioning of the system from the source, thus making it possible to implement modern governance philosophies. After CPC held its 18th National Congress, Xi Jinping ingeniously developed a road map for governance, with a supporting framework and operational schemes as the bases for modernizing governance in China.

First, he needed a road map. The governance system is the culmination of the political, economic, and social systems of a nation. Differences in the political system, the history, and a country's goals will result in different choices in the national governance system. There is not yet a model for governing a socialist country, therefore the fundamental question is still what kind of governance pattern to choose. This is a matter of life and death. Fully aware of the importance of the matter, Xi Jinping pointed out that to improve China's governance system, it must be clear that the governance system is compatible with the state system, with the level of economic and social development, and with the needs of the people. He stressed that Chinese socialism must be upheld as a core principle. Guided by these thoughts, the Third Plenary Session of the 18th CPC Central Committee nailed improving governance and governing capabilities as the goal of furthering reform in all areas. The goal of modernizing governance is to improve and develop Chinese socialism. It will be realized by integrating the governing system and governing capabilities, by ensuring the exercise of the governing capabilities through institutional support, and by improving the governing system through strengthened capacity building.

Second, he needed a framework. Based on the "state-society-market" structure of governance, a multifaceted governance system has been set up with public power at the core. By sorting out the authority and responsibility between government entities, an administrative structure has been established with improved division of duties, and compatible authority and responsibility that check and support each other. The decisive role of the market in allocating resources is being expanded, in order to improve China's market economy. In terms of a national governance mechanism, a multilayered coordinating mechanism has been set up with the participation of multi-governing bodies, which ensures effectiveness and coordination between the different bodies, and transforms single-body management into a joint effort. Coordinating, supervising, promoting, and supporting one another, these bodies have contributed to an efficient and transparent governance pattern.

Third, he needed the operational scheme. Guided by the goals of national governance, an operational scheme has been developed to support the top-level design with plans, measures, and procedures. First of all, more specific plans should be made regarding the institutional arrangement and legislation for economic, political, cultural, social, and ecological progress as well as Party building. Second, to build a service-oriented CPC and government, the regulations and operation framework must be clarified to set up a new intensive governing mechanism under the central leadership and with layered administration, so that central and local governments could dutifully perform their functions, and that governance is carried out with higher efficiency. Lastly, building an operational system with scientific decision-making and resolute implementation. Execution must be enhanced on the formulation of rules, implementation of rules, and accountability, and timely adjustments must be made to correct any variation and ensure execution of the regulations. Designing, coordinating, implementation, and supervision should be closely connected and operated with efficiency.

Strategy two: higher level of governing capabilities

National governing capabilities refers to the ability to govern state and social affairs in a systemic manner. Improvement in the capacity comes from an advanced and scientific system, and an efficient governing body. Without any of the three factors, progress will not be possible. Since CPC's 18th National Congress, Xi Jinping has effectively promoted the level of China's governing capabilities by improving the operation of the government and capability of the governing body, with concerted efforts from all sectors.

First, he needed to improve the governing capabilities and lay a solid institutional foundation. Only under an advanced system can the governing capabilities be fully exercised. Since 2012, to improve the performance of the governance system, China has taken a series of measures to enhance and reform the system, to reflect the change of the times and lay a solid institutional foundation. First of all, in key areas of paramount concern to the CPC and the country, and in aspects that affect future development, deliberation is made at the plenums of the CPC Central Committee, in a way that old rules are abolished before new ones are set. The Decision of the Central Committee of the Communist Party of China on Some Major Issues Concerning Comprehensively Deepening the Reform, approved at the Third Plenary Session of the 18th CPC Central Committee in 2013, is about breaking systemic and institutional barriers curbing economic and social progress through institutional arrangements. The Decision of the CPC Central Committee on Major Issues Pertaining to Comprehensively Promoting the Rule of Law, passed at the Fourth Plenary Session of the 18th CPC Central Committee, sets the guidelines and baseline for implementing the rule of law through institutional arrangements. The Suggestions of the CPC Central Committee on Developing the Thirteenth Five-Year Plan for National Economic and Social Development, adopted at the Fifth Plenary Session of the 18th CPC Central Committee in 2014, points out the direction for establishing new guiding thoughts, and for scientific and sustainable development in the long run. Second, closely focusing on the problems and prioritizing the tasks, the CPC has made a number of plans to reform national defense and the military, SOEs, public security, people's courts, and people's prosecuting bodies, addressing key issues hindering reforms and development in support of the governance system. Finally, when establishing any new system or improving an existing one, attention should be paid to the system's legal support, its coverage and guiding role, feasibility and effectiveness, and accessibility. It should be noted that the compulsory nature of the system must be upheld to ensure authority. Through continued improvements of the systems and institutions, China is marching towards the goal of building a modern, complete, and efficient governance system.

Second, he needed to improve government operation and governing efficiency. National governance largely lies in the efficiency of government operation. Three things are needed to build a modern governance system: Complete and well-established institutional arrangements, an organizational system of effective coordination, and an operating mechanism with effectiveness and flexibility. In the last few years, institutional innovation in government operation has been carried out at all levels, with such goals as building a service-oriented government, transforming government functions, releasing market potential, and boosting social vitality. First of all, transformation of government functions. To build a service-oriented government that is acknowledged by the people, actions must be taken to transform government functions from administration to services, and to modernize the capacity to govern and serve the people. With the people's well-being as the starting point and the main goal, the government must strengthen its function of public services, and improve the basic public service system in order for governments at all levels to help create a sound environment for development, provide good public services, and guard social fairness and justice. Next, the market plays a decisive role. In handling the relationship between the government and the market, well-balanced and well-designed development must be upheld to transform the growth model. It is strictly prohibited to manipulate the market with administrative leverage, or to overrule the economic rules with government action and the will of a high office. Intervention and misplaced administration of the market, and failure to act on the part of the government must be addressed, and the government must stop acting in the place of market forces, stop monopolizing market power, and stop allocating market resources. By introducing equal access, maintaining fair competition, and regulating law enforcement, concrete improvement has been seen in the modern market system. Lastly, streamlining administration and delegating powers to lower levels. Real efforts must be made in delegating powers to lower levels, in streamlining administration, in reforming public institutions, and in promoting the role of social organizations. The functions, positioning, and responsibilities of the government, market, enterprises, and society, and their relationships, have been sorted out, contributing to the separation of government functions from enterprise management, from public institutions, and from capital.

Third, he needed to catch up with modern governance standards, and enhance the capabilities of core governing teams. In the final analysis, national governance is performed by the core governing teams. In China, the governing capabilities have yet to catch up with the governance system, and there is a lack of interaction between the two. The problem is the various bodies taking part in governance, especially the core groups, are not capable enough in executing governance functions. Their failure to catch up with the times has also restricted the development of Chinese socialism, and of the CPC and the country. Xi Jinping is keenly aware that without proper execution and modern governing ability, no system will ever work. Therefore, he has sent instruction to the entire CPC asking officials and leadership members to improve their political awareness, education level, and governing ability as soon as possible, and asking the CPC and state entities, enterprises and public institutions, people's organizations, and social organizations to enhance their working capacity as soon as possible. At the Fifth Plenary Session of the 18th CPC Central Committee, Xi reiterated that with expanding areas of development, more detailed labor division, closer interaction between domestic and international organizations, officials must employ professional thinking and methods in their work; they must conduct studies and research, improve themselves through practice, strengthen the ability to utilize market rules, laws of social development, and the laws of nature, and become experts in leading economic and social development. Since 2012, China has initiated personalized education and training for officials, helping them to be more confident and competent in adapting to the new situation and new tasks.

Strategy three: governance through multiple channels

It is determined by the scope, complexity, and nature of governance that it cannot be done through a single method. Instead, a holistic approach should be adopted in terms of the guiding thoughts, methodology, and measures to promote governance through multiple channels. China has, in the last few years, been accelerating its practice of governance from the aspects of the rule of law, democracy, and society, in accordance with Xi Jinping's governance philosophies.

First, he needed to encourage governance by the rule of law. "People will have no constraints in a country without law, and a country will see no stability without fair law." Dedicated to systemic research on building a nation with the rule of law, Xi has always held that an "order by the rule of law" conforming to the requirements of economic and social development must be established in contemporary China, so that the economy, politics, culture, and social life will all be integrated under the rule of law. Since 2012, Xi has made law-based governance a key principle in the Four-Pronged Comprehensives Strategy. He has developed thoughts such as "The lifeline and authority of the Constitution lies in its implementation," "Governing by the Constitution is a prerequisite for national governance; the key to law-based governance lies in governing by the Constitution," and "The rule of law provides key support to the governance system; it is the institutional basis for the system and the only way to modernize the system." The Decision of the CPC Central Committee on Major Issues Pertaining to Comprehensively Promoting the Rule of Law, approved at the Fourth Plenary Session of the 18th CPC Central Committee, further expounded on the connection between the rule of law and political theories, logic, and stances, and explained the relationship between CPC leadership and socialist rule of law, setting a cornerstone for a new stage in respecting the authority of the Constitution and implementing the rule of law under CPC leadership.

Second, he needed to encourage democratic governance. Democracy and the rule of law are two indispensable components in modernizing governance, and the ultimate goal is democratic governance based on the rule of law. In democratic governance, stakeholders, i.e., the people, the National People's Congress (NPC), and the Chinese People's Political Consultative Conference (CPPCC), will engage in in-depth governance. Through democratic consultation, stakeholders will have more channels to express and ensure their interests, so that the entire country will be an integrated interest group in national governance. Since 2012, China's practice of governance mainly focuses on ensuring that the country is run by the people, and on improving the system of the People's Congress, the system of multi-party cooperation and political consultation led by the CPC, and the system of regional national autonomy and community-level self-governance. Increasing attention has been paid to improving democracy and enriching its forms. Decision-making inside and outside the CPC is more scientific, the depths and widths of democratic governance are strengthened, and the transparency of governing procedures is enhanced—the superiority of the socialist system is showing vigor and strength.

Third, he needed to encourage social governance. Social governance is the foundation of governance; a weak foundation will directly lead to instability. After CPC's 18th National Congress in 2012, significant progress has been made in strengthening and innovating the government's social management function, and a social management mechanism has been developed with social coordination, public participation, and legislative support under CPC leadership. To appropriately handle the relationships between government and society and between the central government and the local governments, and to address the role of citizens in social coordination, efforts have been made in the following areas: Improving social policies, and establishing a mechanism to ensure social fairness in terms of authority, opportunities, and rules; building a modern social organization system, and separating government administration from social management, clarifying the powers and responsibilities, and promoting self-governance pursuant to the law; improving community-level services with network management and socialized services, and expanding social governance channels; improving social risk management, and strengthening the public security system, to exercise dynamic management from the source, and cultivate the ability to respond to emergencies.

Strategy four: the art of governance and techniques

The quality of governance determines its performance and effect. Factors affecting governing quality include the system, execution, personnel, and technology. It can be said that modern technology has become a prerequisite for well-implemented governance, and supports governance. Since 2012, China has strengthened the supporting role of information technology and intellectualism in governance, enhanced the development and application of governance techniques, and promoted the central role of intellectuals in governance. In this way China's governance system and governing capabilities have witnessed rapid progress, and the driving force of technology and intellect is propelling the country.

First, it worked toward perfecting the art of governance. The modernization of national governance is a dynamic process, requiring enriched content and new techniques. Strengthening research on this topic and applying the results in practice will reduce blindness, one-sidedness, and subjectivity to the largest extent. After 2012, more effort has been put in the study and research of governance techniques, and a sound environment has been created to promote the art of governance. The national leadership sets a good example by widely soliciting opinions, especially from experts, during decision-making. Departments

directly under the central government and local CPC committees have followed this example, and scholars and experts are
devoting themselves to the research of governance techniques,
producing a variety of valuable results in support of well-balanced decision-making and development.

Second, it worked toward promoting governing capabilities
with technology. In today's world, with fast-developing science
and technology, people's thinking, their work, lives, and ways of
acquiring knowledge are profoundly influenced by the application of the Internet, cloud computing, big data, and other modern information technologies. New technology is also pushing
governance patterns to change and upgrade. To keep up with
the changes, Xi has launched a series of programs to promote information technology, big data development, and the Internet+
strategy, in an effort to reform governance through technical
progress. The wide application of cutting-edge technology has
changed the governing pattern, brought governance to a new
level, and increased the governing capabilities.

Third, it worked toward setting the future direction of governance. Under the growing influence of information technology, principles guiding the development of governance should
keep up with the times, and set a future direction. It is urgent
to address such problems as mechanical public decision-making, inefficiency of public services, and isolation of information,
and cultivate a driving force for improved governance. In 2012,
Xi Jinping encouraged Shanghai to transform into a smart city
and called upon the entire nation to practice smart governance.
Smart communities, factories, cities, government, and other innovative concepts are now being implemented across the country, promoting modern governance to new heights.

Top-level design, modern governance, and information
technology have contributed to the planning of China's governance road map, consolidated its governing capabilities, enriched its innovation and practice and strengthened technological support to governance. Their implementation ensures

balanced and effective governance, exploring a new path for modernizing the governance system and governing capabilities.

III Igniting an Internal Driving Force of Reform and Innovation

Strategies

- Laying a foundation through promoting new thinking and innovation
- Achieving breakthroughs by focusing on key links
- Relying on the people to further reforms
- Making innovation-driven development a national strategy

Reform and innovation are the two main engines for the evolution of human society. According to Karl Marx, after products take the "dangerous leap" to become commodities, they must continue to improve and innovate to realize large-scale production. The same applies to nations, political parties, and peoples, in a matter of life and death. Xi Jinping knows that in the case of China, a nation determined to go its own path, there is no future without reform and innovation. Since CPC's 18th National Congress, the new generation of CPC leadership, with great political courage and resolve, made innovation-driven development a national strategy, pushed reforms in key links, and made significant achievements in reform by relying on the people. All these have instilled the nation with strength and vigor for further growth.

Strategy one: laying a foundation through promoting new thinking and innovation

Change in the way of thinking heralds innovation; it is the most profound form of reform. For a long time, bound by the agrarian tradition and the doctrine of the average, and affected by the planned economy, the Chinese had not been able to keep up with the times and the goal of building a strong nation, due to an unwillingness to innovate, reform, and pioneer new paths. Xi Jinping saw that the biggest problem hindering reform was nothing more other than outdated ways of thinking. If left unaddressed, China will be abandoned by the times, its humiliating history in modern times will repeat itself, and the result would be disastrous. After taking over the steering wheel of the CPC, the state, and the military, Xi put most of his time and energy into promoting change in the way of thinking in the CPC and the nation, which caused exhilarating clashes between the old and new.

First, he wanted to emancipate the mind. Liberating the way of thinking must come first, or it will be difficult to pinpoint problems, make breakthroughs, create anything new, or form an innovative environment. Xi has made emancipating the mind a main task in breaking established notions, posing challenges to old thoughts, old school, old concepts, and old patterns. Xi took the initial lead to emancipate the mind in the CPC. As soon as he took office, he took on the responsibility of leading the people to explore new thinking, and as a role model, initiated a new campaign to emancipate the mind in the entire CPC. After its 18th National Congress, the CPC has put forth a series of new theories, strategies, and measures, all positive results of the new thinking campaign. Currently, the nation is breaking out of the constraints of outdated thoughts, rigid frameworks, and set patterns, and begins to make judgments based on objective laws and conditions. Xi also takes the lead to apply theories in practice. Emancipating the mind is not a slogan, nor empty words, and no one is allowed to bend the rules. New thinking must be applied in practice to guide actions. Xi pointed out that the key is to take concrete action to address tough problems. Lastly, Xi takes the lead to guide the CPC in emancipating the mind. Courage, endurance, and tenacity are indispensable in pursuing new thinking, and only a strong desire for innovation and exploration will continue to facilitate the drive.

Second, new thinking leads to innovation. The way of thinking decides the path to take. Since its 18th National Congress, the CPC has been making efforts to deepen its understanding of the laws of governance, of socialist construction, and of the development of human society, forming a series of new theories and strategies on governance. The change in thinking has created a favorable environment for expanding the scope, channels, and methods of innovation. New thinking in the economic sector has changed the old practice of a GDP-only criterion to achieve sustainable growth. From protecting the ecological environment, to the New Normal of the economy, then to the five philosophies of development, new ways of thinking have inspired a change of mind and innovation in development. New thoughts on the economy have directly triggered theoretical revolutions in the areas of politics, society, culture, the military, national defense, and diplomacy. These thoughts have become national strategies, guided policy-making, and inspired reform measures, playing an important role in innovation at the state level.

Third, he wanted to inspire innovation through institutional breakthroughs. Institutional change is a prerequisite for innovative vitality. Without institutional change, innovation would not be possible. After CPC's 18th National Congress, the Chinese people have opened up their minds to new thoughts. Institutional innovation has never been so active, and the entire nation is embracing new ways of thinking, with breakthroughs in enhancing organizational flexibility, improving the guidance of various interests, diversifying risks, attracting competent professionals, and cultivating an innovative culture. An industry-university-research collaborative mechanism has been established to encourage innovation in these sectors. A mechanism to guide interests has been set up through policy support to improve innovation. The state has also initiated mechanisms to diversify risk and guide the docking of innovative activities and the capital market, to award outstanding professionals so that their values are recognized, and to cultivate an entrepreneurial culture that tolerates failure, encourages adventure, and is open and inclusive. These institutional breakthroughs are stimulating China's innovative nerve.

Strategy two: achieving breakthroughs by focusing on key links

Many problems and obstacles are blocking China's path to realizing the Chinese Dream and fulfilling its people's wishes. A systematic approach must be taken to clear the way. Since reform will overhaul the distribution of interests, power and the system, strategic planning is needed to ensure that reform is carried out in a forceful and effective manner. Since 2012, Xi Jinping has exhibited the courage of a reformer and the vision of a strategist in leading the CPC and the country to carry out reforms, focusing on key links, to make overall breakthroughs.

First, he focused on the most challenging areas. Reform in the most challenging areas is usually very sensitive, requiring extra effort in political and policy coordination. It is closely connected with the state and political system, intertwined with interest and power, and involves various sectors and individuals. In today's China, among the many tough areas of reform, the most difficult has to be the reforms in the political system and the personnel management system. In the past few years, China has implemented reforms in these two areas on an unprecedented scale. To begin with, reforming the system of power distribution and restriction, and solving such fundamental problems as the structure, operation, constraints of power and the supervision over its execution. Efforts have been made in sorting out the logic of power operation, in regulating the exercise of political power, and in clarifying the reform framework of the political system. Secondly, reforming the administrative system, transforming government functions, innovating the pattern of administration, and improving the structure of the government in order to coordinate the role of the government and the decisive role of the market in allocating resources, and improve the quality and efficiency of governance. Thirdly, reforming the system of punishing and preventing corruption, establishing a long-term mechanism to fight corruption, and ensuring integrity and clean governance among leading officials. Fourthly, reforming the personnel management system. Under CPC leadership, a modern and efficient official selection system has been established to include the standards, examination, and selection of officials, with efforts made in developing a management system, in improving the departments in charge of personnel management and in building a reserve team of officials. Now, preliminary breakthroughs have been made in the promotion and demotion of officials.

Second, he focused on areas of greatest public concern. These areas usually concern the immediate interests of the people, affect the basis of CPC governance and social stability, and are directly linked to societal changes. Right now public concern in the country is focused on reforms in relation to people's well-being and social reforms. After 2012, China, in putting the people first, carried out social reforms to improve their well-being, emphasizing equal benefits to all citizens. In reforms concerning the well-being of the people, attention is being paid to areas such as education, employment, income distribution, housing, social security, and medical care, all of immediate concern to the people, and a series of new policies has been introduced to bring solid benefits to the people. In social reforms, efforts are being made to improve the modes of social governance, in terms of innovating the social governance system, correctly handling social contradictions, and building a public security system, to coordinate governance at the national level and self-governance at the community level. Efforts have also been made in the following areas: Expanding the channels for the people to express their concerns, resolving disagreement among the people, maintaining social stability, improving public security in communities, and ensuring an orderly social environment. A harmonious and stable society is the best testimony to the starting point and ultimate goal of reforms tailored for the people.

Third, he focused on key links. Reforms in key links directly affect the overall progress and effects of reform, and play a guiding role in the reforms of other areas. In China, economic reform is of paramount importance, with market-oriented reform and the reform of SOEs at its core. Following CPC's 18th National Congress, China has stepped up to promote market-oriented reform. By letting the market play a decisive role in allocating resources, efforts have been made in delineating the border of the government and the markets, cultivating and developing a market system, allowing market access, strengthening market supervision, clarifying the entities in market competition, building a fair, efficient, and orderly supply system, and promoting more efficient allocation of market resources. Supporting reforms have been carried out in the taxation and financing system and the building of free trade zones, to lay the foundation for marketization, strengthen the growth capacity of the economy, and transform the growth model, in preparation for further reforms. A new round of reforms has been initiated at SOEs, aimed at preserving and increasing the value of SOEs, increasing the competitiveness of the state-owned economy, and amplifying the functions of the state-owned economy. The measures taken include innovating the management of state-owned assets, implementing category-based management of SOEs, improving the modern corporate system, promoting restructuring of SOEs and mixed ownership reform, exploring a salary distribution system applicable in the market economy, strengthening CPC leadership over SOEs, further improving the vitality, control, influence, and risk-resisting capacity of SOEs, making them firm pillars in the economy, and consolidating CPC's economic base.

Strategy three: relying on the people to further reforms

The people are the drivers of China's endeavors. That is why China's reforms must serve the people, rely on the people, and benefit the people. This is decided by the fundamental principle that the CPC must wholeheartedly serve the Chinese people, and by the nature of Chinese socialism, and must not change under any circumstances. Since 2012, China has held to the principle that reform must be people-oriented, that the people's dominant role must be upheld, and that their pioneering spirit must be applied in action.

First, reform must concentrate on people's needs. The fundamental goal of comprehensive reform is to consolidate the people's dominant role, respond to their concerns, and meet their needs. In the past few years, the CPC and the government have regarded the people's needs as a top priority, addressing problems that are of pressing concern to the people, and putting the people's interests first. Clear goals have been set under this direction. In the Decision of the Central Committee of the Communist Party of China on Some Major Issues Concerning Comprehensively Deepening the Reform, approved at the Third Plenary Session of the 18th CPC Central Committee, the CPC took full consideration of the people's concerns, and put forth a series of major reform measures to bring benefits to the people and improve their well-being, striving to ensure their economic, political, and cultural rights. The effort has welcomed warm responses from the people.

Second, reform must incorporate people's wisdom. The people are the true heroes, in whom true wisdom and strength reside. Continuing reform in all areas is a grand endeavor, an ongoing cause, and faces countless difficulties, obstacles, as well as uncertainties. Its success lies in the originality of the people and their wisdom. The CPC has been putting in extra effort on investigation and research, asking officials to go to the people, obtain first-hand information, and seek effective solutions to problems. Experience is drawn from the practice of the people and developed into reform measures in order to address the concerns of the people. By introducing an open-door approach in developing new policies, the CPC is able to gain an understanding of the people's needs and their concerns. Through a mechanism to solicit opinions from various channels, policy-making has become more targeted, efficient, and pragmatic. The Internet and new technology are being utilized to establish online platforms for the people to access policy-making, and a bridge has been built for fast and direct communication between the ordinary Chinese and CPC decision-makers.

Third, reform must pool people's strength together. The people are both the beneficiaries and practitioners of reform. To promote further reform, the people must actively engage in the creative activities of reform, and they must be fully mobilized to form a strong force of reform in the entire society and the entire nation. Since CPC's 18th National Congress, the CPC leadership has emphasized the people's dominant role in pushing reform, and greatly inspired their enthusiasm in supporting and participating in the reform drive. Through strengthened education on and interpretation of the significance of reform, the people have come to realize its importance, and become staunch supporters. Through education in the proper handling of the relationship between the state, collective interests, and personal interests, on the correct understanding of short- and long-term interests, and on a clear understanding of the pains and rewards of reform, people have become firm followers, supporters, and promoters of reform. Through strengthened efforts in mobilizing and organizing the people to take part in reform, in developing a social participation system, and in relying on the CPC and social organizations, the people have united as one to devote themselves to the reform effort.

Respecting the people's will, soliciting their opinions, and gathering their wisdom, the CPC has won the utmost understanding and support of the Chinese in carrying out reform. The people's originality and creativity in driving reform is instilling new energy in the cause.

Strategy four: making innovation-driven development a national strategy

Since 1978, when the reform and opening-up drive was introduced, China chose an investment-driven mode of development with consideration of its resources endowment, and it was proven as a correct choice based on the national conditions and the need for fast growth. With the advent of the third industrial revolution, China has entered a transformative phase, and the old growth pattern is no longer productive. Faced with the difficulties in choosing a new path, Xi Jinping, after in-depth research, had come to the conclusion that to adapt to the new age and catch up with the rest of the world, China must rid itself of the overdependence on the material factors of production, as required by the traditional development model, and switch to a new growth engine driven by innovation, to build an internally-driven dynamism of development. In this way China will be able to develop unique advantages as a latecomer, build momentum for lasting growth, and take the initiative to gain the high ground. After CPC's 18th National Congress 2012, China made a timely adjustment to promote the innovation-driven mode of development as a national strategy, deepening innovation at a higher level and laying a solid foundation for further growth.

First, it consolidated two pillar projects to lay a strategic foundation. Any form of innovation is based on study and research. During the development of an innovation-driven strategy, Xi Jinping put extra emphasis on studying and soft-science research, two pillar projects, to promote research and innovation and support the new strategy by building new-type think tanks. On the one hand, he called on the CPC to study, research, and build study-oriented organizations, and to improve the capacity to acquire new knowledge. He said that "rivers and seas are what they are by embracing streams," and that "a nation must study to progress." By carrying out the studying project, China strives to expand the vision of its people, enrich their knowledge, promote their professional development, and enhance their ability to apply advanced knowledge and technology, in order to bring up a highly capable reserve of professionals. Progress has been made in this regard since CPC's 18th National Congress. By promoting study and research in the CPC and the society, the people have been motivated to create a social environment of innovation; by building an Internet-based and personalized education system of lifelong learning, more innovative talents have been cultivated; and by improving the educational level of the Chinese, the nation's innovation capabilities has been enhanced. On the other hand, building think tanks at the national level has been made a priority. Addressing difficulties in reform calls for strong intellectual support. Therefore, more efforts must be made to build think tanks with Chinese characteristics, in order to promote scientific and democratic decision-making, modernize the governance system and governing capabilities, and increase the soft power of China. Since 2012, Xi has been vigorously pushing the development of think tanks in China, with marked progress in terms of new thoughts, achievements, and team building. It is expected that with the birth of professionals and high-end think tanks, their research results will be widely applied to help with national governance, and contribute to China's innovation-driven strategy.

Second, it strengthened technological innovation. Just as study and research constitute the two pillars of an innovation-driven strategy, technological innovation serves as the strategy's key link. In this global arena of technological innovation, as Xi Jinping puts it, China cannot afford to wait or act slowly, and that it must make technical innovation a core task for rapid implementation. First of all, a series of new ideas on technological innovation is now leading the drive, greatly inspiring scientists to carry forward the spirit of innovation, ignite technical innovation through reform, and explore an independent path of scientific and technological development. Secondly, the principles and direction of technical innovation have been decided. To create a healthy environment of innovation that encourages the pioneering spirit and tolerates trial and error, efforts have been made in these areas: Facilitating the transformation of research results into products, stimulating creativity by strengthening the role of scientists and researchers, and following the proven rules to improve the efficiency of innovation resources allocation. Thirdly, progress has been made in the following aspects: Focusing on key areas of technological innovation, promoting the integration of technical innovation and socioeconomic development, strengthening the capacity of independent innovation, improving the mechanism of career development, and expanding the scope of technical cooperation. Under these initiatives, new technological achievements have reached a new record with unparalleled creativity and vigor of innovation.

Third, it enriched the value of the innovation-driven strategy by comprehensive innovation. Centered on the critical task of technological innovation, efforts have also been made in promoting comprehensive innovation in terms of management, organization, brand development, and business model, in coordinating military-civilian integration, and in introducing foreign expertise and helping Chinese businesses go global, in order to achieve the organic and coordinated development of technological and institutional innovation, to optimize the value of the innovation-driven strategy, and to drive development. After CPC's 18th National Congress, China, by making breakthroughs in key areas, has been able to advance technological innovation in all respects at an unprecedented level in terms of intensity, velocity, depth, and width. To begin with, building a "chain of institutions," by improving the environment for innovation, and creating favorable conditions and providing institutional support to comprehensive innovation through systemic, organizational, and managerial innovation. Next, building a "chain of collaborations," by establishing an innovative system led by technological innovation and integrating efforts from industries, enterprises, the market, products, operation, and management. Lastly, building an inclusive policy support system, creating an innovative ecology, cultivating a culture of innovation, promoting entrepreneurship in society, and converging energies from all sectors to promote economic and social development.

While promoting continued reform and innovation and building the momentum for development, China is striving to reform its ways of thinking to achieve breakthroughs in key areas, relying on the people to promote and implement the innovation-driven strategy. The people have emancipated their minds, and with great enthusiasm for further reform, they are contributing to solving the tough issues deterring reform, and laying a solid foundation for future development. Key problems addressed, a bright future is lying ahead with promises of more vigorous growth.

IV Mustering Strength from All Walks of Life for National Rejuvenation

Strategies
- Ensuring the people's well-being and uniting the people
- Peaceful development and mutual benefit
- Upholding core values and inspiring positive energy
- Promoting positive guidance and mainstream thinking

To ensure lasting stability in a country, it is indispensable to have a well-designed system, a political party in service to the people, state-of-the-art governance, and united effort from all fronts. Today, when economic globalization is accelerating and the domestic interest pattern is undergoing profound changes, it is not an easy job to maintain China's stability and positive momentum. It requires the people's support, a stable international environment, and favorable public opinion. In governing China, the CPC must hold to the principle that "the world belongs to the people," and uphold justice, serve the people, and integrate into the world, to create a magnetic field of positive energy.

Strategy one: ensuring the people's well-being and uniting the people

To have the people's support, the CPC must strive to improve their well-being, which affects the future of China. Programs concerning people's livelihood reflect the capacity of the governing party, and only those who have the support of the people will remain in office. China is a populous country with a large territory and many different ethnic groups. It has always been challenged with the imbalances between ethnic groups, urban and rural areas, and different regions. As the effort to build a moderately prosperous society strengthens, the people are developing higher expectations for a good life, which poses new challenges for the government. Taking on these challenges, the CPC leadership, by ensuring that the fruits of reform and development benefit all citizens, is working hard to address the weaknesses and enhance the advantages, implementing a series of projects to reduce poverty, handle tough issues, and bring benefits to all the people. With these efforts, the CPC has effectively united the people as one.

First, it instituted the "basic living" project. The basic living project refers to a social security network that ensures minimum living support for the impoverished, disadvantaged, special groups, and poor ethnic households. After CPC's 18th National Congress, China has been striving to provide basic living support to marginal and most needy groups, so that they could live in dignity and seek development. The measures taken include improving old-age insurance, basic medical care, and social relief, to build a system of minimum living management. Specifically, efforts have been made in the following areas: Improving basic medical care, strengthening medical relief and special relief, supporting disadvantaged seniors in rural areas and unregistered and unemployed persons in urban areas, exempting financially challenged students from tuition and fees, and helping low-income persons enhance job skills and seek employment. All these measures have enabled minimum living standards for the neediest groups, including them in the social security network. It has demonstrated the governing party's concern for disadvantaged groups, and the superiority of the socialist system.

Second, it instituted a project to bring benefits to all. Aimed at meeting the people's growing material and cultural needs, the project is a comprehensive and sustainable effort to benefit all Chinese citizens, and ensure equal access to the fruits of development. The project is based on relevant policies of the CPC and state, and is an indicator of national strength and the people-oriented governing philosophy. Since 2012, centered on increasing the supply of public services, and addressing the most immediate concerns of the people, efforts have been made in the following areas: Improving infrastructure and the ecological environment, strengthening social governance, and enhancing the quality of public services; improving education quality and the balanced development of compulsory education, and ensuring equal access to educational resources; promoting employment and entrepreneurship, and encouraging business startups to promote employment; narrowing the income gap, strengthening the adjustment of redistribution, and adjusting the national income distribution pattern; building a fairer and more sustainable social security system, including adding all citizens in insurance plans, and improving the insurance system; promoting public health, deepening reform in medical and health services, and building a basic medical care network covering all urban and rural areas; and improving housing conditions, building a housing supply system, and ensuring basic housing for all citizens. A basis for lasting stability and a source of domestic demand, the project has become a pillar program to improve people's well-being, effectively enhancing the quality of people's lives.

Third, it instituted a project to eradicate poverty in China. With the goal of lifting China's remaining 70 million people out of poverty by 2020, the project poses many tough challenges considering the timeframe, budget, and the number of people under the poverty line. It has a vital bearing on the final stage of building a moderately prosperous society in all respects, and on the quality of Chinese socialism. In recent years, the CPC leadership led the entire party to fight a battle of "targeted approach to alleviating poverty," to ensure that no one is left behind on the path to prosperity. With careful planning, efforts have been made in the following aspects: Strengthening policy support, implementing the policy based on categories, reducing poverty by providing development opportunities and through allocation, education, and medical relief, and mobilizing the entire society to take part, to ensure that not a single household or an individual is left behind, and that poverty is completely driven out of China. The project to eradicate poverty is the final barrier on China's way to common prosperity. Its success will go down in history as another accomplishment of the CPC.

The three projects, carried out in coordination, have formed a vigorous network for the people's well-being. It has significantly increased the cohesiveness of the CPC and the country, and united the Chinese people around its leadership.

Strategy two: peaceful development and mutual benefit

China is deeply integrated with the world. The world cannot do without China, and China cannot grow without a favorable environment and the understanding and support of the international community. With inclusiveness, a positive image, and the courage to take on responsibilities, China will win more friends on its way of development, and gain strength from them for the rejuvenation of the Chinese nation. Since 2012, CPC leadership has set up a good international image, presenting China to the world, expanding its influence, and contributing to global growth.

First, China embraced the world with open arms. Three decades have passed since China introduced the reform and opening-up drive in 1978, yet there is no end in pursuing further opening-up. Today, economic globalization is bringing overwhelming changes to the world, in terms of commerce, information, technology, human resources, and culture. This is why China must integrate with the world with a modern and inclusive mindset. After 2012, China has stepped up its opening-up initiative. First, it set up a positive image in global exchanges, making friends and introducing China, telling China's history, and making China's voice heard. Second, it promoted international cooperation, expanding the scale of economic opening-up, practicing reciprocity and sharing of benefits, promoting opening-up in both ways, building strategic trust, enhancing mutual benefit in trade, and strengthening cultural exchanges and integration at deeper levels. Lastly, it let the world witness China's inclusive culture, and know about its stance of dialogue instead of confrontation, and friendship instead of alliance. United, the global community will grow stronger; isolated, it will only weaken itself. No one will ever develop behind closed doors, and no one is allowed to take advantage of others in the name of development.

Second, China took on responsibilities and contributed to global development. As a major developing country, China should play its part, take on responsibilities commensurate with its status, and making its voice heard. In the last few years, China has been actively engaged in the building of a world community with a shared future, contributing its part to the effort. Specifically, it has taken the following measures: Politically, building a global partnership featuring consultation and equality; in the area of security, building a security mechanism to ensure fairness and justice, and joint development and mutual benefit; economically, seeking openness and innovation, and inclusiveness and reciprocity; culturally, promoting cultural exchanges featuring harmony in diversity and an all-embracing attitude; and environmentally, building an ecological system that respects nature and seeks green development. China has played its part in the handling of international affairs. First, it has dared to air its views and uphold justice. Abiding by the international norms and upholding justice, China stands firmly against hegemony and power politics, opposes dominating the weak or bullying the small, and has always held to principle and justice. Second, it has actively participated in international affairs. Its involvement in international affairs enables China to perform its international obligations and meet its development needs. China actively promotes reform in the international governance system, advocates multifaceted development for developing countries, facilitates the docking of development strategies between different nations, seeks pragmatic development, improves the global development framework, and strives to promote fairness, justice, cooperation and mutual benefit in the international order. In terms of specific affairs, China does not avoid its responsibilities, and has always held to its pledges as a large country. Lastly, it has provided relief in times of crisis. China plays an important role in international relief efforts. In light of these conditions, China regularly relieves the least developed countries of their debts and provides assistance to these countries, and takes an active stance in poverty reduction cooperation, ecological protection, and medical and educational training. With these efforts China is sending practical and concrete help to these countries, assisting them in turning the table around.

Third, China has expanded its international influence. The nature of international relations is best reflected in realpolitik. To have one's voice heard on the international stage, it has to be strong. This does not mean "fist" and "muscle" in the traditional sense, but the comprehensive national strength combining the soft and hard powers. After the CPC held its 18th National Congress, China has been working hard to improve its comprehensive strength, which has effectively boosted its international influence. First, it has showcased the hard power. China has shown the world its achievements in the reform and opening-up initiative, its industrialization drive, and the strong growth in its national strength. There is no end to the reform and the opening-up drive, and measures have been taken in these areas: Implementing the Belt and Road Initiative, founding the Asian Infrastructure Investment Bank, selling the Chinese high-speed rail overseas, and proposing to build an Asia-Pacific free trade zone. These have brought Chinese benefits and opportunities to the world, showcasing China's progress and expanding its influence. Second, enhancing soft power. Through cultural exchanges and bilateral activities, China is striving to present its advantages, offering examples of its development, and disseminating Chinese culture worldwide, integrating its soft power with the world and showing the world what it can do. Lastly, it has used the smart power to expand influence. China adopts a holistic approach to combine the forces of the economy, capital, ethics, and culture in handling international disputes and diplomatic affairs. By offering both opportunities and plans, exercising flexibility in utilizing resources, and integrating soft and hard powers, China has significantly strengthened its global leadership.

Strategy three: upholding core values and inspiring positive energy

Without morality, a nation cannot prosper, nor can people find their place in society. In national development, core values constitute the most enduring and strongest forces. As the "state philosophy," they are also the soul of a nation's soft power, and determine the culture and direction of the country, embody the spirit of the people and nation, and reflect the value standard of a society. With no common core values, a country will not be able to decide what is right, and its people's behaviors will have no guidance, making it impossible to progress. For the future of the country and the people, Xi Jinping attaches great importance to the core socialist values, stressing ethical progress while seeking economic growth so that the nation can find its soul and discover its roots.

First, he has worked to establish core values and unite the people. China is undergoing substantial social transition, and the diversity in ideology and values is growing. In the last few years, cultivating core socialist values has been made a priority, a cornerstone for uniting the people and mustering their strength. First, the strategy focused on prosperity, democracy, civility, and harmony at the state level, guiding the CPC and the society to form shared values, and encouraging all Chinese to fight for the common goal. Second, it focused on freedom, equality, justice, and the rule of law at the social level, guiding innovation in social governance and building a modern society, and promoting a social ecology that is honest, fair, just, and positive. Third, it focused on patriotism, diligence, honesty, and amity at the individual level, guiding all citizens to follow moral codes and codes of conduct, and improving personal qualities. This system of values that integrates the state, society, and individuals is conducive to cultivating the core socialist values, promoting the Chinese culture, and realizing the Chinese Dream. The core values will undoubtedly become embedded in Chinese genes and support the great rejuvenation of the Chinese nation.

Second, he has worked to implement education campaigns on core values. Cultivating a value system requires the unity of knowing and doing, as one will only practice what they believe. The knowledge about core values comes from education, a process to enhance knowledge and recognition, and to promote them to the entire society. It takes long periods of time for any value system to become mainstream, not without frustrations and setbacks, and constant adjustment must be made in the ongoing process. Specifically, the adjustment should be carried out at both the organizational and personal levels to ensure the correct direction. After the CPC held its 18th National Congress, Xi Jinping has been paying extra attention to the role of education, public opinion, cultural environment, practice and implementation, and institutional guarantee in cultivating core socialist values, so that the values are applied in all social sectors and in guiding the people's conduct. Internalized to guide their actions, the core values have helped the Chinese people to adjust and improve themselves.

Third, he has worked to encourage the practicing of the core values. The development of core values relies on education and practice, the latter being the foundation. The key to practicing the core values lies in action on the part of the people. Only in this way can the people be equipped with the core values for practice. The CPC leadership has, in recent years, been striving to promote the practice of the core socialist values, spreading the campaign to its entire rank and file. First, strengthening organization and exercising unified leadership over the campaign, and issuing the Action Plan for Cultivating and Practicing the Core and Socialist Values, was a bold step towards effectively implementing the core socialist values. Second, focusing on the key links, helped promote good models set by leading officials, and set standards for society. In the meantime, deciding on the targets and contents of the campaign, basing the campaign in families, schools, communities, and offices, and employing such methods as family education, education programs, and interaction and joint effort, so that the core values are internalized by the people and the society to nourish their growth. Third, building a long-term mechanism, focusing on the guiding role of policies and laws, and formulating regulations and rules on professional integrity and standards by promoting codes of conduct in cities, industries, and enterprises, and among urban citizens, villagers, and students. Efforts have also been taken in building a social credit system, and in strengthening legislation, law enforcement, and supervision, to practice core socialist values in the long term.

With these campaigns, China's positive traditions and philosophies, which advocate self-cultivation, integrity, harmony, and unity, have been further inherited and promoted. The people are now more capable of correctly handling the relationships between the state, society and citizenship, and a fair and just social environment is taking shape.

Strategy four: promoting positive guidance and mainstream thinking

In this great time of progress, society needs a positive mainstream mindset. In realizing the rejuvenation of the Chinese nation, there must be correct guidance on public opinion, otherwise no joint effort can be formed. Xi Jinping has clearly seen that without a common goal, a nation is just a heap of loose sand, and nothing could ever be achieved. In recent years, China has made continued efforts to promote the correct direction of public opinion, ensuring that the CPC and the people firmly hold to the guiding role of mainstream thinking.

First, it has provided positive guidance domestically. In the age of openness, information, and media, different schools of thinking, opinions, and cultures interact and clash with each other. Faced with a complicated situation, the CPC is challenged by questions such as how to consolidate and expand mainstream thinking, how to guide the people to differentiate the mainstream from minor branches, how to look through the surface and see the true nature, and how to focus on the positive instead of the negative. Since 2012, China has been implementing a positive guidance policy domestically, holding to the leading thoughts and the correct direction amidst deviating torrents, and forming a strong positive force. Solidarity and positive thinking have been made the principles to guide the effort, which has effectively defended the core basis. First, it has encouraged adhering to mainstream thinking, ensuring the timely and widespread coverage of mainstream voices, and turning the media into platforms to disseminate the voice of the CPC and the government, showcasing the mainstream culture of Chinese society, and delivering its opinions publicly. Second, keeping up with the times in terms of information dissemination, innovating new media management, enriching forms of dissemination, applying new technology, and building new platforms, to improve the capacity and quality of positive guidance. Third, it has responded to public concerns and hot issues, preventing and controlling the spread of rumors, extreme views, and negative thinking, and paying equal attention to cultivating positive energy and managing negative thoughts and opinions, so that erroneous thinking cannot spread to cause damage, and that mainstream thoughts take command.

Second, it has introduced China to the world and set a positive image. The more open a nation grows, and the more it integrates with the world, the more important international communication becomes. International communication is a kind of transcendental effort, which is linked to a country's soft power, to the quality of its global integration, and to national security and state interests. After the CPC had its 18th National Congress, with his unique vision and observation, Xi Jinping has been paying special attention to this communication effort, making such initiatives as disseminating Chinese culture, introducing China's development and changes, enhancing its rights of speech, increasing its global presence, creating an external environment to help its growth, and consolidating the defense line against hostile ideological forces. First, it accomplished these things by clearing up misunderstandings, and letting the world know the real China. International communication poses great challenges due to political and cultural differences, and only with action can progress be made. The West's misunderstanding of China has had a long history, and it is a fact that China is at a disadvantage compared to the West in terms of publicity. To address the issue, China has stopped being overly modest, a traditional Eastern trait, and become more confident in introducing China's economy, development path, and opportunities. It has shown to the world China's confidence in its path, theories, system and culture of the country, and the world, in turn, has developed a deeper understanding and fairer judgment of China, giving China growing international support. Second, it has improved its ability and strategy in promoting international communication. The world does not fully understand China's development path, nor can it completely appreciate China's stories or its philosophies. Among the many reasons that led to this situation, the biggest problem is China's failure to explain itself to the world. Since 2012, China has been strengthening the capacity building for international communication, and based on shared values, striving to form a discourse system that relates both to China and the world. Emphasis has been put on such complementary pairs as principle and artistry, purpose and strategy, depth and amity, so that the world develops an interest in China's stories, hears China's voice, understands China's propositions, and in the end, trusts China as a good partner in global governance. Third, it has kept to the baseline and won respect. With the upgrading of media technology, foreign hostile forces are using the Internet to infiltrate China, causing growing threats to the country's stability and security. Recently, China has made Internet security a top priority on its agenda, exercising effective guidance over the direction of public opinion and addressing major emergencies involving information security, and attaining firmer control over the nation's ideological basis. On hotspot issues, China is making its voice heard in a stronger fashion, resolutely rebutting malicious attacks such as "China threat" and "China collapse," firmly safeguarding political stability. It has also strengthened the management of the Internet through effective measures. By these efforts, China is making headway in its international publicity campaign, creating a brand new image as a responsible socialist country in the East.

Third, it has cultivated positive energy through communication. For decades, communication has been a traditional advantage of the CPC. Under the new circumstances, to realize the Chinese Dream, the CPC must carry forward this tradition, inspire and encourage people with correct theories and thoughts, and cultivate positive energy in the country. In recent years, the CPC has carried forward the good tradition of communication, and improved its contents according to the needs of the new situation, enriching it with new advantages. Education and establishing models are two important strategies. In educating all citizens and improving their moral qualities, efforts have been made to publicize positive examples which unify the people. By innovating the forms of education, progress has been made in strengthening the theories of Chinese socialism and the core values, in enhancing the education on the Chinese Dream, the Four-Pronged Comprehensives, and other new thoughts and strategies. In setting good examples and models, much work has been done to select model figures from all sectors, and efforts have also been made to establish correct values, set standards of the times, and include the model figures in the soft power system. A profound environment for learning from role models has been formed across China.

The ultimate goal of uniting the people, exhibiting China's charms, cultivating positive energy, and consolidating mainstream thinking lies in serving the Chinese Dream, in exploring the strength for its realization. With a unified nation and a firm foundation, China will definitely make further progress in achieving its goals. In the past, the CPC had secured victories in the revolution, nation building, and reform by winning people's support; there is no doubt that in the new era it will continue to create miracles by relying on the people.

Of strategic, systemic, holistic, and guiding importance, Xi Jinping's governance philosophies have been successfully steering the direction of future development with a clear head, leading national development with modern thinking, igniting an internal driving force of reform and innovation, and mustering strength from all walks of life for national rejuvenation. In this system of key focuses and a layered structure, political stability addresses the fundamental direction of national development, well-designed and well-balanced governance deals with the operation of the nation; reform and innovation brings vitality and energy to development, and the effort to improve people's well-being consolidates the basis of further growth. The practice of China's reforms will continue to prove the well-balanced nature, strict logic, practical basis, and resourcefulness of Xi Jinping's governance philosophies.

CHAPTER THREE

Practice of Xi Jinping's Governance Philosophies

Key Phrases

Xi Jinping's practice on governance in the past few years can be understood at three levels:

- Outstanding characteristics of the practice
- Philosophical bases of the practice
- Far-reaching influence of the practice

In the few years after Xi Jinping took over CPC leadership, including the political and military work of China, he has made significant achievements in governance, showcasing his governance philosophies and strategies at different levels and on different facets. By analyzing these accomplishments and strategies, it is not difficult to come to the conclusion that Xi's national governance philosophies have developed into a complete system, exploring the path and laying the foundation for future development. Studying the philosophies behind Xi's national governance, finding a pattern of the strategies, analyzing the supporting factors, and reflecting on the practice's influence on the future is an urgent task for forming a clear understanding of his theoretical system of governance, and for deepening the entire CPC's understanding of his philosophies. It will be conducive to revealing the intellectual support behind the practice and strengthening the collective authority of the CPC leadership, to enhancing the people's confidence in following CPC's leadership, and to opening a new chapter of Chinese socialism with one heart.

I. Outstanding Characteristics of the Practice

Characteristics
- Abiding by objective laws
- Starting from China's realities
- Focusing on top-level design
- Making concerted efforts from all sectors

Xi's governance philosophies in practice cover these areas: reform, development, and stability; domestic affairs, foreign affairs, and national defense; and those in relation to governing the CPC, the state, and the military. It is incorporated in the nation's politics, economy, society, culture, ecology, legal system, and diplomacy.

There is no doubt that these past few years have witnessed the emergence of new thoughts on governance, the people's aspirations and expectations, and the improved governing capabilities and many achievements. Responding to the changes of the times and addressing the root problems, Xi's governance strategies will serve as a golden key to solving China's problems at the current stage and in the near future, and to answering the question of the future of socialism.

With a few years of practice, the governance philosophies have developed into a system. Its main contents are: in pursuit of the Chinese Dream and aiming at the Two Centenary Goals, coordinating and pushing forward the governance of the CPC, the state, and the military, implementing the Four-Pronged Comprehensives Strategy and Five-in-One Strategy, continuing to modernize national governance, and building a modern socialist country in all respects.

Xi Jinping's governance philosophies and its practice have four features.

Abiding by objective laws

In putting forth new philosophies, thoughts, and strategies on governance, Xi has always abided by objective laws, discovering them and summarizing them for application. His remark that "we cannot step on a watermelon rind and let it slip us around" vividly tells the principle that governance must abide by objective laws. In practice over the past few years, he has been leading the new generation of CPC leadership to deepen its understanding of the laws of CPC's governance, of building socialism, and of the development of human society. Bold steps have been taken on this basis.

In following the laws of governance by communist parties, the CPC adheres to four principles: First, CPC's leading role in political, military, civilian, and educational affairs in all regions; second, CPC leadership is pushing forward all reforms and development plans; third, improving CPC's governing capabilities, enhancing the people's trust and support for CPC governance, and consolidating the legitimacy of CPC governance; fourth, strengthening Party building, maintaining the advanced nature and purity of the CPC, and improving its cohesiveness, competence, and charisma.

In following the laws of building socialism, the CPC has four convictions: First, in the superiority of socialism, and in the fact that only socialism can save China, and we must develop it and make it strong; Second, in the path, theories, and system of Chinese socialism, which is a choice made by history and the people, and has been proven by facts; Third, in CPC's ability to renovate itself, and in its capacity to uphold openness and inclusiveness, to learn from the achievements of other countries, and to improve itself and make the most out of the superiority of socialism; Fourth, in the firm faith of Chinese socialism, and in that the nature of socialism is never to be changed while the approach can be renovated. The CPC will not fall back on the old path with closed doors, nor will it abandon the banner of socialism. It will continue to explore a path of Chinese socialism that keeps up with the times.

In following the laws of development of human society, the CPC adheres to four principles: First, incorporating China's development globally, following the laws of the development of human society while exploring its own path, providing the world with China's wisdom and plans, and integrating China with the rest of the world; Second, coordinating productive forces and productive relations, freeing productive forces through reforms at deeper levels, improving productive relations through institutional innovation, and addressing the incongruities between them; Third, innovating the way of thinking, practicing the strategy of innovation, coordination, green development, opening up, and sharing of benefits, ensuring that the development is innovative, open, harmonious, featuring cooperation and competition, and bringing mutual benefit, and continuing to power the development of human society; Fourth, promoting people-oriented and inclusive development, emphasizing the actual needs of the people, bringing the fruits of economic development to all citizens, ensuring that the people share a common responsibility for development and are equally entitled to opportunities and benefits, and enhancing the sustainability and inner vigor of growth. It is also important to put people first, safeguard social fairness and justice, and promote the harmonious development between man and society and between man and nature.

Starting from China's realities

In pursuing development, the CPC has always put people

first, starting from realities and seeking truth from facts. Since the CPC held its 18th National Congress, this principle has guided Xi Jinping's governance practice. On the one hand, he puts people at the center of development in all areas, focusing on the people's well-being and their living standards as the ultimate goal. Holding to the principle that the development is for the people and by the people, and the benefits are shared by all people, China has been following the laws of economics, nature, and society to pursue sustainable, scientific, and inclusive growth, exploring new patterns of political and economic progress. On the other hand, Xi takes the global situation into full consideration, as well as the specific conditions of the CPC and the country, when making decisions, driving reforms, and seeking development. He has not forgotten the fact that China is still in the primary stage of socialism. This is a country with 5,000 years of history, a population of 1.3 billion, and a party with 87 million members; however, there are 70 million people living under the poverty line even though it is the world's second largest economy. He has always attached importance to the integration of history and current realities, theories and practice, form and content, paying equal attention to China's historic heritage, its developmental path, political experience and principles, the current demands and realities, and future plans. Xi's governance philosophies and strategies are an answer to the requirements of the times, a response to China's current stage of development, and a source of vitality and strength.

Focusing on top-level design

At a time when China has entered a transitional stage and is in the most difficult phrase of reform in a complicated international environment, it has started addressing the long-time shortages in top-level design and strategic planning, carrying out systemic designing and planning focused on the problems and aimed at future development. Measures have been taken to sort out the guidelines and strategies of governance, to get a clear understanding of the problems and challenges blocking the way, to strengthen the coordinated and systemic implementation of different reform measures, and to form a holistic solution that integrates different components and coordinates different stages in order to address the fragmented and contradictory policies, to prevent damage caused by ineffective policy and misused time and money, and to explore a path of governance based on top-level design and preemptive planning that can best release the potential of macro policies.

In the last few years, China has been pushing forward reforms in the economy, politics, military, culture, and society, strengthening CPC discipline, rigorously implementing the rule of law, governing officials with strict discipline, and setting new guidelines, policies, and measures in all sectors. These policies and measures, in particular, are closely interconnected, catering to both the overall and detailed situations, key areas and general issues, and urgent and regular tasks, presenting a new pattern of governance that is orderly, properly organized, well-paced, and coordinated.

Making concerted efforts from all sectors

On the basis of top-level design and coordinated planning, more effort is made to coordinate the implementation of the guidelines on governance, so that the whole nation will make concerted efforts to promote the initiative at all levels. First, this is done by focusing on the common root of the interests of the nation and the people. Second, short-term and long-term interests are coordinated. Third, reform, development, and stability are integrated. Fourth, the governance of the CPC, the state, and the military is carried out in a holistic manner. Fifth, the rule of law and the rule of virtue are combined. Sixth, equal attention is paid to material and cultural progress. Seventh, China's development globally is integrated. Since 2012, China has enacted a series of reform measures that balance and enhance each other, significantly increasing the joint effects of the measures. China has entered a new stage of achieving moderate prosperity, its reforms making headway to deeper levels, the rule of law being implemented across the nation, and the CPC run with strict discipline. These achievements are witnessed by the people, contributing to the realization of the Chinese Dream. A new pattern, underlined by systemic and orderly planning, has been formed.

The aforementioned features are connected with and enhance each other, illustrating the systemic, targeted, and effective nature of national governance strategies. Abiding by objective laws ensures that the governance of China follows the correct path; starting from realities ensures that the governance of China will not lose vitality; focusing on top-level design ensures that the governance of China enjoys strategic advantages; and making concerted efforts from all sectors ensures that the governance of China is implemented in an effective and orderly manner. These characteristics have been developed to address the core concern of national governance, and have infused its practice with vitality and creativity.

II. Philosophical Bases of the Practice

Philosophical Bases
- Unity of CPC conviction and personal integrity showing the way
- Integration of knowledge and practice guaranteeing the foundation
- Combination of guidelines and methods ensuring the results
- Solidarity of leadership and people strengthening the nation

An analysis of Xi's governance philosophies must start from the practice and the philosophical core which supports the practice. Since 2012, Xi's successes in practicing his governance strategies largely come from the philosophical bases, which have ensured the direction, efficiency, and accomplishments in the governance of China. If we compare Xi's governance skills to a giant tree, then its philosophical bases provide the nutrition for its growth.

Philosophy is a discipline about wisdom, and about the essence of the times. It is a prerequisite for being a leader. Practice has proven that the higher the office is, the higher the demand is for one's philosophical knowledge; and that a good leader usually has strong philosophical training. The Chinese Dream, the practice of Chinese socialism, the goals of governance, the risks and challenges in this time of transformation, and the highly integrated global pattern all call for stronger and more modern philosophical bases in the Chinese leadership. Only in this way can it steer China on the correct path efficiently and vigorously, and govern and develop China.

Xi has always regarded philosophical knowledge as an essential life lesson, a "source of wisdom" for the mind, a "golden key" to performing official duties, and a "true skill" in governance. With perseverance and diligence, he has greatly enriched his philosophical bases, and developed unique ideas on governance. In practice, through the skillful application of the four bases of conviction and integrity, knowledge and practice, guidelines and methods, and leadership and people, he has improved governance philosophies, ensuring that it is on the right track, based on research, highly efficient in realizing goals, and is propelled by an inexhaustible source of energy.

Unity of CPC conviction and personal integrity showing the way

The CPC's role as China's only governing party has determined that China's governance always be on the correct path, which relies on the strong conviction in the CPC's mission. The conviction of Chinese Communists is the culmination of man's integrity, and points to the direction of the development of human society. Personal integrity is the basis of conviction in the CPC and enhances the conviction. Only by integrating the two can the CPC have a stronger foundation. By applying Marxist principles, Xi guides practice with a philosophical system that integrates conviction and integrity, ensuring the correct political direction of the governance of China.

Again, it is essential to combine CPC conviction and personal integrity in the practice of national governance. Efforts have been made to promote conviction in CPC members as an integral part of Party building, and personal integrity as a way to enhance recognition and inheritance of the traditional culture, so that the two can interact and integrate to ensure a strong political and cultural basis for governance. Since the CPC held its 18th National Congress in 2012, Xi has developed a holistic approach to integrate the strengthening of CPC leadership and the inheritance of traditional Chinese culture, laying a solid theoretical, historical, and cultural basis for CPC leadership. In coordinating national development, he has combined economic development with cultural progress, so that they complement and support each other; in pushing law-based governance, he has integrated the rule of law with the rule of virtue, so that national governance enters a sound development path with both the law and virtue at work; in global governance, he has balanced the interests of the nation and the people with openness and inclusiveness so that China's opening-up drive keeps to its principled operation and leads to mutual benefit; and in building up a governance team, he has combined political and personal education, in order to build a team of officials with firm political convictions, personal integrity, honesty, and righteousness. The wide application of the approach has laid a strong cultural basis for the political direction of Xi's governance strategies, effectively strengthening CPC leadership, implementing its guiding principles and policies, executing its plans and decisions, and ensuring that actions are taken to help realize CPC's goals.

Combining CPC conviction and personal integrity cultivates character. The key to the cause of the CPC and the country lies in the people, and the key to governance lies in the officials. If officials, the "key minority," are not reliable as CPC members and in personal integrity, it would lead to fatal consequences in China. That is why attention must be paid to strengthen the education of officials in politics, theories, and personal integrity, in order to ensure long-term stability in China. We must admit that for a period of time, some CPC members and officials have been severing and antagonizing CPC convictions and personal integrity, either ignoring the cultivation of good conduct, or falsifying or discarding their beliefs in the CPC. Unaddressed, this problem will severely harm the CPC and the country, and shake the foundation of CPC's governance. Keenly aware of the consequences, Xi Jinping has seen that without personal integrity one's conviction will not be able to stand up to the test of an emergency, and that traditional culture should be a source of nutrition for integrating the efforts in promoting political conviction and personal integrity. On the one hand, great efforts have to be made to actively build an integrated educational system to strengthen CPC members' convictions and beliefs, principles, and discipline comprehensively. On the other hand, much work has to be done in cultivating such virtues as fairness, righteousness, modesty, diligence, endurance, and magnanimity in CPC members, to facilitate their growth and the awareness of their mission. In the entire CPC, members and officials are working hard towards achieving these goals as they improve their overall qualities.

Integration of knowledge and practice guaranteeing the foundation

The unity of knowledge and practice is a cornerstone of the Marxist theory of knowledge, a basic principle and methodology of dialectical materialism. By applying Marxist theories in governing China, Xi Jinping has put the emphasis on practice, stressing theoretical innovation to guide practice, and developing a cycle of practice and knowledge, thus ensuring his governance practice is on the right track.

Freeing people's minds and starting with facts, can enhance the strategic planning of governance. An open mind guides social development, and only with an open mind can people develop new ways of thinking, and achieve economic prosperity and social development. Yet freeing up the mind does not mean disregarding the national conditions, imagining things behind closed doors, or recklessly experimenting without guidance. Attention must be paid in order to appropriately handle the relationships between freeing up the mind and seeking truth from facts, between overall progress and key breakthroughs, between top-level design and prudent planning, between bold strategies and steady steps, and between reform, development, and stability. In a developing country with a large population like China, any disregard of the realities of the country, the development stage, and the governing party will inflict immeasurable losses, and might lead to mistakes that could ruin all efforts. Since 2012, Xi Jinping has kept a clear head on this matter of principle, opening up the mind while holding to the baseline, taking proper measures, and correcting mistakes. He is resolute on the fundamental principle of CPC leadership, leaving no room for negotiation or dispute, and promoting CPC leadership in all areas of governance. For example, he emphasized that no matter how far the reform has gone, that CPC leadership is critical, that "the CPC leads all sectors in all regions." Fully aware of the fact that China is still in the primary stage of socialism, he develops plans based on a consideration of China's realities, and divides the strategies into different stages, emphasizing that the goals be made based upon capacity. He opposes sending excessive foreign aid beyond China's ability, and stresses research and measurement of capacity before making any development plan. In economic and financial reform, he instructed that pilot programs be run before large-scale implementation, and that programs that are not effective, or have caused public opposition and are badly operated, be delayed or terminated. For example, during the reform of the financial system, the "circuit breaker" mechanism for the stock market, which did not meet the expected performance standards, was called off just four days after its implementation. When adjusting the industrial structure, the term "supply side reform" was changed to "supply side structural reform," a timely response based on research.

Knowing the laws and patterns and solving difficult issues, can enhance the targeted practice of governance. The correct understanding and application of laws and patterns is the prerequisite for solving problems, and also a Marxist principle that must be upheld in national governance. Any practice disregarding the laws and patterns will be blind and reckless, and is destined to fail or even lead to severe consequences. In his practice of governance, Xi has skillfully mastered the laws of man's development, of the primary stage of socialism, and of the main problems in the current stage of development, making targeted plans, strategies, and tasks for the problems in different stages. First, based on the full understanding of the law of the development of human society, and of the current situation of the Chinese society, Xi proposed the Two Centenary Goals, the Four-Pronged Comprehensives Strategy, and the Five-in-One Development Strategy, providing strategic guidance to solving China's pressing problems in the current stage. Second, mastering the law of the primary stage of socialism and adopting a historical perspective, he divided the six decades of China's development into two stages: 30 years of independent exploration and 30 years of reform and opening up. Based on facts, Xi analyzed the continuity and differences between the two stages, acknowledging the value of the setbacks and guiding people to use objective judgment on the history of Chinese socialism. He emphasized that building Chinese socialism must start from the biggest reality that China will be in the primary stage of socialism for a long time, providing a correct theoretical basis for governing China and showing the utmost respect for the laws of the primary stage of socialism. Third, based on China's problems in the current stage, Xi was able to solve many pressing problems by mastering the laws and patterns of politics, the economy, the military, culture, and Party building.

Combination of guidelines and methods ensuring the desired results

A complete cycle of knowledge and practice involves the stages of thinking, theory, and practice, and whether the correct theories could develop into correct guidelines, directly determines the effects of the practice. Furthermore, the guidelines and methods must be integrated to ensure the best results in practice. Xi Jinping pays special attention to applying the Marxist theory of methodology in guiding the implementation of top-level design and strategic planning, and has formed his unique methods in national governance. For example, setting targets based on people's needs, making overall plans with strategic thinking, exploring paths with pragmatism, enhancing vitality with innovation, addressing problems with dialectical thinking, mustering strength with systemic thinking, fending against risks with baseline thinking, and achieving benevolent governance with the rule of law.

It is essential to pay equal attention to the focal points and both sides of things. Mao Zedong, Deng Xiaoping and members of the older generations of CPC leadership were all good at handling the relationships between the focal points and the two sides of things, one of the most important fruits of Marxist theories. Like them, Xi Jinping also has a deep understanding of dividing things into two or more aspects for analysis and decision-making, striking a balance between them instead of choosing one side. Every aspect is taken into account: The favorable and the unfavorable, the opportunities and the risks, and the more cautious approaches and top-level design. Xi also stresses the internal connections between things, focusing his effort on the main problems, and addressing both the overall development and key areas. In the face of complex situations and tough tasks, he first decides on an overall strategy to address all problems, and then takes priority in solving the main problems before taking care of the rest. Since 2012, Xi has been paying great attention to ensure that governance strategies are more systematic and coordinated, emphasizing holistic designing and the main problems, such as running the Party with strict discipline, the judicial responsibility system, technological innovation, and building a strong army, showcasing the importance of integrating focal points and different sides of things.

Paying equal attention to principles and flexibility is always of great importance. According to Marxist dialectical materialism, the contradictory sides of all things depend on each other and oppose each other. This determines that in handling different relations, equal attention must be paid to principles and flexibility, to comprehensive knowledge rather than partial understanding, and to adjusting to the changes rather than sticking with old practices. In handling CPC and state affairs, Xi Jinping has exhibited outstanding skills and understanding of principles and discipline, and flexibility in application, fully demonstrating the integration of principle and flexibility. On matters of principle, he is resolute and never backs off: The announcement that Chinese socialism "will not repeat the old path, nor deviate from the right path," the firmness in deepening the reform "in areas that must be reformed while adhering to the fundamental principles," the resolve in the "zero tolerance" of corruption and running the CPC with strict discipline, the support to the governance of the Hong Kong and Macao special administrative regions in accordance with the law, and the bottom line of safeguarding national sovereignty and interests. President Xi is also flexible enough to take into consideration the realities and specific conditions of the present time. When dealing with the question of Taiwan, considering that the two sides across the Straits have been separated for six decades, he offered a flexible solution under the One China framework, expressing the willingness to "negotiate with the Taiwan side on an equal footing, and make reasonable arrangements." This led to the historic meeting of the leaders from both sides of the Taiwan Straits, which has illustrated that the One China policy is the guiding principle in handling the Taiwan question, and that a certain degree of flexibility should be exercised in cross-Straits relations. In diplomacy, Xi has also put forth pragmatic and effective guidelines and strategies, making room for China's diplomatic endeavors in a new era.

Solidarity of leadership and people strengthening the nation

Leadership and the people have always been an integral entity. Lenin once pointed out that the leadership is a comparatively stable group composed of selected people, those who are the most prestigious, influential, and experienced, to take the most important offices. Mao Zedong said, "Only the people are the driving force to create world history," and "The people are the true heroes." These remarks explained the important positions and roles of the leadership and the people from different perspectives. In the relationship between the leadership and the people, the leadership not only leads the ruling party, but also the people with the two groups' interests and goals highly identical. Without a leading core, a political party and a nation could hardly form a unified will or a degree of cohesiveness that prevents the party and country from falling apart. Likewise, without the people's practice and support, the leadership will lose its leading status.

In China, the integration of leadership and the people is determined by the fact that the CPC is the only governing party and the leading core of China's various undertakings, by the CPC's principle of wholeheartedly serving the people, by the objective laws of the development of human society and China's practice, and by the people's leading role in creating history and the CPC's good traditions. The leadership and the people play the two major roles in applying Marxism in China's reality and they are inseparable. Only in this way can the people become the true leaders of China, which is the root of a Marxist political party. The CPC has always upheld the integration of the leadership and the people. After 2012, Xi Jinping, a visionary statesman and a courageous worker, has ensured the key role of the leading figures and the people in creating history, creatively developing historical materialism by integrating the functions of leadership and people to a new level.

Strengthening top-level design ensures the integration of the leadership and the people. The integration of the leadership and the people falls not only into the realm of philosophy, but also into practice. To ensure effective integration, the leadership must first take the helm in top-level design, to form the guiding thoughts, plans, policies, and mechanisms that are conducive to this effort. In the last few years, Xi has personally overseen the development of major strategies concerning reform, the rule of law, and economic and social development, so that the CPC, the state apparatus, the leadership, and the people work for common goals and interests. Wholeheartedly serving the people, the CPC exercises its power endowed by the people and for the people. Focused on the people's needs, governing strategies have been developed to ensure that the people are always put first when promoting reform, the rule of law, and economic progress. Focusing on problems of pressing concern for the people, targeted and systemic measures and mechanisms have been formed to promote the development of the people, to ensure their access to benefits, and to encourage their creativity.

In implementing CPC's principle of staying in close touch with and relying on the people, it is made clear that the people are at the core of promoting reform and development, that they take the main role in applying their creativity, and that their deputies duly represent them at national congresses, in order to strengthen the ties between the CPC and the people.

Setting good examples and joining forces ensures the integration of the leadership and the people. Under the new historical conditions, the changing mindset of the people, their rising expectations and concerns, and their new ideas pose difficulties for integrating them with the leadership. This requires innovation in the methods and channels. In his governance practice, Xi Jinping has always set good examples for CPC members, officials, and the people. Diligently performing his duties as the top leader of the CPC, the state, and the military, Xi has resolutely taken on the responsibility of leading the Chinese people towards the rejuvenation of the Chinese nation, never hesitant in making decisions, mapping strategies, and voicing ideas on key issues. His personal integrity, good image, and high standards have set a perfect example of a leader who devotes himself to his nation, his party, his country, and his people. President Xi attaches great importance to the people, going to the people, relying on them, mobilizing them, and guiding them to balance their own interests with the interests of the nation, to incorporate personal pursuit into the cause of the CPC and the state, to keep up with the leadership in thinking and action, to safeguard the authority of the leadership, to follow the guidance of the CPC, and to strive with one heart for a better China.

III. Far-reaching Influence of the Practice

Impacts
- Setting a good image of the CPC and consolidating its governing basis

- Forming a governance system and pioneering the path
- Building a strategic framework of governance and opening up new grounds
- Consolidating the efficient governing model and expanding systemic advantages

The past few years have far-reaching influence on China's future. President Xi's accomplishments in governance and his new ideas and strategies not only benefit China now, but also future generations. The practice of China's governance has proven that the country is entering a new era of vitality and prosperity. It is foreseeable that the guiding principles and policies that are being executed now will exert lasting influence on future development. We have reason to believe that the valuable experience and theoretical advances will play a central role in opening new grounds of governance on a higher level, and in guiding and promoting the practice to deeper levels. Analyzing Xi's achievements on the governance of China over the past few years, it is certain that his governance philosophies will profoundly contribute to China's future development.

Setting a good image of the CPC and consolidating its governing basis

The CPC is the leading core of China's development. The victory of the revolution, the success of nation building, the breakthroughs of reform, and the achievements of development have proven that the good image of the governing party ensures success and a bright future. But we must see that after six decades at the steering wheel, the CPC is increasingly faced with the danger of estrangement from the people. It is undeniable that the CPC's image has been tainted by a few corrupt officials who have undermined its reputation and damaged its image in the people's hearts. Xi Jinping has clearly seen the danger of this key political issue and the harm it could do to the Party's solidarity.

After CPC's 18th National Congress, with confidence, courage, resolution, and integrity, he has taken action to strengthen the cohesion of the Party and the people, implementing the Eight Regulations, carrying out campaigns against the Four Forms of Decadence, pulling up unspoken rules from the roots, combating corruption with strong measures, promoting clean governance and integrity, and guarding social fairness and justice. All of this has restored people's confidence and trust in the CPC. The Party's effort to restore its image has gained people's trust, and won their support for the next level of governance.

First, the Political Bureau of the CPC Central Committee sets a good example by implementing the Eight Regulations. The effort to restore the CPC's image starts from its Central Committee, which has taken the lead in all major campaigns, including the education program of the Party's principle of staying in close touch with and relying on the people, the three guidelines for ethical behavior and the three basic rules of conduct, the fight against the Four Forms of Decadence, and the improvement of Party conduct. All these efforts have enabled the people to see that the leadership is taking action and is of one heart with the people.

Second, the zero tolerance of corruption shows CPC's resolve to address its problems. Just two months after the CPC convened the 18th National Congress, the first "tiger," a corrupt high-ranking official, was arrested and investigated. The intensity of the campaign was never before seen: there is no cap to an official's rank that protects against investigation nor any limit at lower levels. Everyone is equally subject to Party discipline and the law; no one is exempt. The tough stance on corruption proved very popular in the CPC and among the people, effectively educating officials at all levels. It has shown the Chinese people that the CPC is confident and strong, and upholds justice, inspiring the people to continue to follow CPC's guidance and leadership.

Third, the CPC ensures concrete benefits for the people.

"The starting point and ultimate goal of our Party and government is to ensure the well-being of the people." "Only the people can judge whether they are living a life of prosperity." "Show the people the benefits of the reform plans, and let them enjoy more concrete benefits." "It is my concern that the impoverished rural population could live better lives." The above remarks were made by Xi Jinping, a man of the people. With the implementation of a more targeted poverty reduction effort, the people have genuinely felt the warmth and care of the CPC and the government. With a bright future ahead, the people are having greater expectations of the CPC.

The people's trust is vital, and those who win the hearts of the people will win the world. The people's support has always been the pillar of the undertakings of the CPC and the country. That is why the strengthened ties between the CPC and the people, the people's rising trust and confidence in the CPC, and the enhanced cohesiveness inside the CPC have consolidated its foundation—the most important impact of Xi's contribution to China's governance.

Forming a governance system and pioneering the path

During the CPC's 18th National Congress, Xi Jinping made the proposition of the Two Centenary Goals, and the concept of the Chinese Dream. Over the past few years, a series of new ideas and strategies have been developed about the governance of the CPC, the state, and the military, and on domestic affairs, foreign affairs, and national defense, which could be summed up as Xi Jinping's governance philosophies. They are the latest achievements of Chinese socialism, and an important component of Marxism.

First, a philosophical system has been developed with governance at its core. As more problems arise in the economy, society, and the environment, the traditional ways of governing the country could hardly keep up with the times. To catch up and face the challenges, and to transform the governing model from administration to governance, China must establish a new system of national governance. Since 2012, the new generation of CPC leadership has been striving to innovate the guiding principles on governing the CPC, the state, and the military, gradually developing a complete system of governance. Under this framework, the Chinese Dream serves as the ultimate goal, with the Two Centenary Goals, the three main tasks of governing the CPC, the state, and the military, the Four-Pronged Comprehensives, and the Five-in-One Development leading the way. Facts have proven that Xi's governance philosophies are guiding the effort to improve China's governance, and will continue to play a larger role in leading the CPC and the state, and in opening up new grounds in governing China.

Second, CPC leadership controls all undertakings in national governance. The CPC leadership is the biggest advantage and essence of Chinese socialism. Today, China's development has reached an unprecedented level in terms of width and depth. With all sorts of interests intertwining, there must be a strong leading core to oversee the country's direction and coordinate all fronts. Xi Jinping has always put CPC's unified leadership as a central task and has formed his governance strategies based on this principle. First, the CPC's leading position has been strengthened under the new situations. Xi pointed out that the CPC must assume leadership over all sectors and in all regions and that CPC's core leading role must be upheld. Under his guidance, the CPC established the important principle that the Party must steer the overall direction, make development plans, coordinate all fronts, balance the interests of different groups, and sort out major relations to ensure its leadership across the country. Second, the Party's work model and methods have been innovated. More attention is being paid to transforming the Party's propositions into national will through legislation, and more emphasis is put on exercising theoretical, political, organizational, economic, and legal means to realize CPC leadership. Lastly, efforts have been made to effectively improve CPC's governing capabilities, stressing that the CPC must exercise self-discipline and be strict with its members.

The governance system with CPC leadership not only inherited CPC's good traditions, but has also developed the framework with consideration of China's new realities. Facts have proven that the key to China's governance lies in the CPC and that, again, its leadership is China's biggest advantage. With the strong leadership of the CPC, China is able to navigate the rough seas with certainty and calmness, to overcome difficulties and create miracles, and to proceed from victory to victory.

Third, supporting policies have been developed to promote economic, political, cultural, social, and ecological progress, and strengthen Party building. Since the CPC's 18th National Congress, under Xi's governance framework, China's economy, politics, culture, society, ecology, and Party building have entered a new era of innovation and improvement. Targeted programs have been developed for all sectors, effectively supporting and enriching the framework and its contents, and serving as important components of the system. The main contents of Xi's governance philosophies include: transformation of the growth pattern, focusing on the "key minority" of leading officials, encouraging traditional Chinese culture and heritage and disseminating positive energy, improving people's well-being, promoting the rule of law, building a society of fairness and justice, implementing green development and never sacrificing the environment for economic growth, and strengthening Party building at the roots and strictly implementing Party discipline in relation to politics, organization, integrity, ties with the people, work, and life. It also stresses strengthening political guidance of the military, strengthening the CPC's absolute leadership over the military, and ensuring that the army is able to fight and win battles.

Clearly layered and complementing each other, the above

three levels are supported by strict logic, theories, and practice. It is safe to come to the conclusion that the system of Xi's governance philosophies has been formed. It has laid the theoretical foundation for governing a modern China with mature strategies and practice, and will undoubtedly exert far-reaching influence on China's future and its development of socialism.

Building a strategic framework of governance and opening up new grounds

The governance of China faces many challenges, reflected in the long-term governance of the CPC, the middle income trap, the trend of globalization, and the fact that China is in the primary stage of socialism. These have determined that China must innovate its governance philosophies, improve the governing system, develop a new-type governing model that is in line with the laws of the development of the governing party, the state, and human society, and establish a governing pattern that is open, inclusive, efficient, and research-based, in order to explore a new path of socialism. Since 2012, China has strengthened the CPC's role in national governance, in an effort to modernize the governing system and the governing capabilities. Focusing on deepening governance and participating in global governance, it is conducive to integrating China's governance into global governance, improving the integral approach of national governance, enhancing its level of practice, and amplifying its effects.

First, it's working to improve the CPC's governing capabilities. Since 2012, the CPC leadership has been focusing on the most stubborn afflictions, pressing problems, and weak links taking resolute measures to regulate the Party with strict discipline, restoring CPC's image and reputation, and winning the support of the people. By improving the ability to solve its own problems, the CPC has strengthened its purity, pioneering nature, and its governing legitimacy.

Second, it's working to strengthen the governance system and modernizing the governing capabilities. At the Third Plenary of the 18th CPC Central Committee, the CPC decided on the ultimate goal of furthering reform as a means of improving and developing Chinese socialism, and modernizing national governance system and governing capabilities. On the one hand, it is improving and innovating the system to better handle the relationship between the government, the market, and the society. In economic governance, it is ensuring that the government regulates the market, and the market guides business activities, and gives play to the decisive role of the market in resource allocation. In political governance, it is ensuring the integration of CPC leadership, the dominant role of the people, and the rule of law, deepening the reform of the political system, and letting the rule of law play the decisive role in allocating political resources. In social governance, it is cultivating and regulating social organizations under the leadership of the CPC and the government, ensuring that social organizations allocate social resources, and letting them play the decisive role in allocating those resources. On the other hand, addressing the incongruities between the governing capabilities and the governing system, efforts are being made to strengthen capacity building of governing officials, improve the efficiency of policy execution, and to form a positive cycle of complementing system and capacity.

Third, China is working hard to integrate its governance globally. The acceleration of economic globalization is ever more closely tying the world together, forming an international community with shared interests. Many problems are no longer confined within one country's borders and many challenges cannot be tackled by one country alone. In the face of severe risks and challenges, no one can stay away and concerted effort is a must to address them. Therefore, China must integrate with the rest of the world to build an open governance system. The governance of the CPC and the country will have to operate on a larger platform and at a higher level. Since the CPC's 18th National Congress, China has been proactively engaged in global governance, creating a favorable external environment for the CPC and national governance, creating a good image for the country and its diplomacy, showcasing Chinese strength, and contributing to global growth and governance—all these have won wide acclaim from the world community. First, China has formed a unique global governance outlook; it upholds an open strategy of reciprocity, practices openness, inclusiveness, cooperation, and mutual benefit, and actively promotes reform and innovation of the system of international economic governance. Second, China has initiated the Belt and Road Initiative, the Asian Infrastructure Investment Bank, and the China-Latin America Forum to set up an international cooperation framework on a broader scale. Through these frameworks, China is able to take the initiative to influence global governance. Third, China has enhanced its international influence: guiding the transformation of the G20 to a long-term mechanism by consolidating its central role in global economic governance, enhancing China's international influence by putting the RMB in the SDR and promoting reform in the international monetary system. Fourth, China is striving to build a new type of state-to-state relations. It has promoted a new-type of China-US relations to solve tough issues in global governance; enhanced China-Africa cooperation and the building of a community based on a shared future between China and Africa; and deepened South-South cooperation and made historic breakthroughs. Over the past few years, China has become an important political and economic pillar globally, and a force that cannot be ignored. China is taking part in global governance with a more confident and active stance, contributing to global development. On the global governance agenda, China no longer passively accepts the rules, but has rather begun to make them, turning itself into a positive contributor and decision-maker.

The governance of the CPC and the country, and global

governance have broken the traditional model of governance, expanded its boundaries, and opened up new grounds for governance in a socialist country in the new era. Xi Jinping's innovation in this regard has left huge room for future development.

Consolidating the efficient governing model and expanding systemic advantages

The CPC is the only governing party in China, the leading core of China's undertakings. It must be seen, nonetheless, that for a period of time the problem persisted as to how to exercise the Party's leading role in an efficient manner. Such problems as insufficient utilization of the Party's political advantages and room for improvement in the strength of Party leadership have directly led to poor implementation of some of the CPC's policies and measures, adversely affecting the practice of governance. Since 2012, CPC leadership has been fully activating the unique advantages of China's political system and the socialist system, creating an efficient operating mechanism that ensures the supremacy of its leadership and pools all strength on major projects. Xi personally chairs the Leading Group for Deepening the Reform and other leadership groups, and by strengthening top-level leadership, coordinating all fronts, allocating resources, and higher levels overseeing lower levels, he has successfully dealt with a series of difficult problems and formed a joint force in improving the efficiency of governance under a complex situation. First, responsibilities are clarified. The person in charge of a unit must take responsibility, concentrating efforts to tackle the toughest issues and ensuring that the leader can be able to solve the problems of his unit. Second, governing efficiency is improved. With the leader taking charge, friction has become rare, so that resources and personnel can be best utilized to reduce the cost of coordination and increase work efficiency. Third, the role of leaders is amplified. The new leading pattern has provided China with an efficient and operational model to solve its problems. This pattern's unique characteristics will release great potentials in its execution, and serve as a powerful weapon to address China's problems.

This new model and mechanism largely came from Xi's resolve and vision, relying on his innovative spirit. It is Xi's contribution to the governance system that has enabled the CPC to further cultivate its political advantages.

Xi Jinping's governance strategies are a living example of the Marxist theories of system, holistic approach, and dialectics. The guidelines and correct decisions have ensured China is marching along the right path, carrying forward its positive traditions, addressing existing problems, and looking into future development. China has ingeniously integrated logistics, accurate planning, and steady promotion, and further developed Xi's governance philosophies in its clear and unique way. China's core governing capabilities are now complete.

CHAPTER FOUR

The Governance of Great Leaders

Key Phrases

The four abilities of great leaders in governance:

- The ability to ensure the correct direction with vision and foresight
- The ability to guide national development through good judgment and command
- The ability to identify and cultivate internal drives for growth and innovation
- The ability to lead and inspire their people to achieve goals

Governance strategies are the culmination of the wisdom and experience of leaders, and for any strategy to work there must be supporting mechanisms at the base. To uncover the laws and trends of governance from the perspective of leadership, we must first study these decisive factors. We must also open up our minds and expand the research to include global leaders, and focus on the common traits of successful governance practices to ensure that the study will yield more reliable and worthwhile results.

When studying the development of society and history, some political scientists pointed out that for a nation to realize stability and prosperity there are seven preconditions: a wise leader, able and efficient central leadership, a set of applicable theories and policies, a complete and authoritative legal system, a powerful army, a clean and hardworking governing team, and a solid network to ensure people's livelihood. It has been proven all across the globe that an outstanding statesman plays a significant role in determining the fate of a country. In its times of crisis, without Mao Zedong, Deng Xiaoping and other great leaders, China would not have gotten where it is today. Likewise, without Abraham Lincoln and Franklin D. Roosevelt, the USA would probably have become a different country. In ancient times and in modern times, in China and in other countries, great leaders have these in common: a broad platform, rich resources, a strong team, an exceptional vision, leading skills, courage and resolve, and personal qualities.

If we conduct an in-depth analysis of outstanding leaders, it will not be difficult to notice the abilities that made them leaders despite the differences in their time, nation, environment, and belief, and despite disparities in their governing strategies, styles, methods, and goals. By analyzing large numbers of examples and cases, we have come to the conclusion that outstanding leading figures are generally good at strategic thinking, using holistic approaches, and taking on responsibilities. They are good commanders and decision-makers, reformers and pioneers, are popular with the people, and have great charisma and influence. Condensed, these qualities can be summed up as "the ability to ensure the correct direction, the ability to guide national development, the ability to identify and cultivate internal drives for growth and innovation, and the ability to lead the people to reach the goal." According to the theory of core leadership capacities, these four aspects are essential in shaping great leaders. From our analyses of Xi Jinping's governance strategies, practice, and achievements, it is evident that the four capacities are fully demonstrated in his designing, planning, and reform measures, which have laid the basis for the theories.

The ability to ensure the correct direction with vision and foresight

Vision and foresight are essential capacities for great leaders and directly determine a nation's direction of development. These qualities are reflected in the ability to look far and aim high, and in the broad vision, quick thinking, and forward-looking planning. It is the ability to see what others cannot see, and do what others cannot do, especially at crucial times and on matters of principle. Great leaders are always able to make judgments based on unique thinking, and take resolute action to solve problems. They are also masters at spotting bad tendencies, summarizing lessons and discovering patterns, and addressing changing times and upcoming trends. For them, strategic thinking and the art of wisdom are equally important.

It is never a coincidence that great leaders have these outstanding qualities, which are based on rich life experience, knowledge, vision, logic, deduction, and resolve. It is the result of many factors at work.

In human history, great statesmen were exclusively those with exceptional vision and foresight. In the history of capitalism, particularly, the 32nd US President, Franklin D. Roosevelt, was a man of such qualities, who exercised effective control over the country's direction. In the face of the Great Depression of 1933, Roosevelt, with a clear understanding of the crisis' nature and sound judgment, made timely adjustments to the failed policies of President Hoover, his predecessor, and launched a basket of new measures to stimulate the economy, create jobs, and regulate the financial market. These efforts eased social tensions, and helped America through the most difficult times. Socialism also had some of the best leaders. Without Lenin's judgment that "socialism will probably make the first breakthrough in the weak links of capitalism," it could have cost the socialist movements more time groping in the darkness. Without Stalin's predictions about the development of WWII, the turning point of the War would never have come and the Soviet people would have suffered much longer under the German Nazis.

In Chinese history, the role of leaders in guiding national development has never been more evident. In the early stages of modern China's development, the country could have gone through more difficulties if not for Mao Zedong's confidence in "starting a fire with a single spark" to carry out the revolution in the 1920s, for his judgment of a protracted war during the fight against Japan in the 1930s, for his planning for China's future during the Liberation War in the late 1940s, and for his conclusion that "only socialism can save China and develop China" in the period of nation building. In the beginning of the reform and opening-up initiative, China could not have achieved 30 years of rapid growth, which led to today's success, if not for Deng Xiaoping's judgment that "a new world war was not possible for a fairly long period of time," and for his decision to shift the focus from war to economic development.

All the strategies and plans Xi Jinping has made after he took over as China's president have shown the same depth of vision on the country's development. Shortly after taking office, he put forth the Eight Regulations, vowing to correct bad conduct and crack down on corruption in response to the most pressing concerns of the Chinese people. He proposed the founding of the Asian Infrastructure Investment Bank, an effort to boost Asia's financial prowess and improve the international financial order, which effectively promoted China's say and influence in the global financial market.

The ability to guide national development through good judgment and command

Leading figures' good judgment and command is central

to controlling the overall situation and implementing strategies. These qualities are mainly reflected in top-level designing, overall planning, exercising of good judgment, problem-solving, organizing and coordinating, and commanding skills. In national governance, good leaders have clear goals, research-based plans, innovative measures, and efficient implementation. They are able to help their nations go one step higher up the ladder in good times, and fend off risks and dangers in adversity, ensuring that their countries always press forward despite difficulties and hardships, and that their people are confident and full of hope in their nations' future. Practice has proven that successful governance lies in the following aspects: first, efficiently transforming the will, wisdom, strategies, and ideas of the leadership into state strategies and plans; second, efficiently transforming national strategies and plans into policies, systems, and institutions; third, efficiently transforming policies and mechanisms into programs and actions. These three transformations are the foundation to ensure strict implementation of central decisions and plans. In China and around the world, great leaders have all ingeniously pushed the integration and smooth operation of these three aspects in governance.

During WWII, Stalin outwitted Hitler with the admirable resolve of a great commander. In 1942, when the Germans were making inroads on the Eastern Front, Stalin evaluated the situation and decided on a massive counterattack there to dampen the Nazi's arrogance. As the commander-in-chief, he personally charted attack plans and commanded the Soviet army in the 200-day Battle of Stalingrad. Claiming 850,000 casualties from the Axis, the battle's victory turned the tables on the Eastern Front, laying the foundation for the final victory.

Mao Zedong was also a skilled military commander, whose leadership not only pushed China to victory in times of war, but also guided national building afterwards. After completing the First Five-Year Plan (1953-1957), China was facing many problems due to the political isolation and economic lockdown imposed by imperialist forces. Realizing that China could never copy the Soviet model, but rather had to explore its own path, Mao heard the reports of 34 ministries and departments, and came up with major adjustments to key national policies, establishing the principle that China must go its own path based on its own realities. He also chaired meetings of the CPC Political Bureau to discuss detailed principles and plans, and published "On the Ten Major Relationships," in which he explained the relationships between industry and agriculture, coastal areas and the inland, state and individuals, national defense and economic progress, and China and foreign countries. This article provided theoretical guidance to building socialism and laid a solid foundation for the reform and opening-up drive, the development of a market economy, and Chinese socialism.

The ability to identify and cultivate internal drives for growth and innovation

The ability of leading figures to lead reform and innovate plays a large role in promoting their countries' progress. These qualities are mainly reflected in their open-mindedness, the desire for innovation and change, the vigilance against rigidities, the courage to face risks and take on responsibilities, the pioneering spirit, and the resolve to tackle difficulties. In national governance, good leaders exhibit great courage and resourcefulness, and the willingness to take challenges, break out of constraints, face sensitive issues, address deeper-level problems, fight against inaccurate mentalities, and push reform in all areas. The ability to reform and innovate is the most evident aspect of great leaders' capacities, because it is a core capacity that works best at inspiring and mobilizing the people. The ability is difficult to develop, though, because it is closely related to the leaders' goals, temperament, life experience, and many personal qualities.

Only through reform can one progress and become stronger.

Thus the ability to reform and innovate has always been a main topic for leading figures. From ancient to modern times, from China to globally, all great leaders have been able to push reform and remain consistent.

In ancient China, Liu Che (156-87 BC), Emperor Wu of the Han Dynasty, was an outstanding reformer. Separate governance of feudal lords had always been a huge problem for the Han Dynasty (206 BC-AD 220), and the efforts of Emperors Wen (202-157 BC) and Jing (188-141 BC) to weaken the feudal lords failed due to strong opposition and weak implementation. However, Liu Che was different. He withstood the pressure from interest groups and took great risks in reforming the system, imposing an edict to abolish the long-standing practice in which the eldest son of feudal lords inherit their fathers' lands and titles, by giving other sons equal rights to fiefdom. In this way, the local powers gradually weakened and disintegrated, losing the ability to challenge the central authorities. With strengthened power, Emperor Wu laid the cornerstone for the prosperity of his reign. His success could be attributed to the parallel reforms of politics, the economy, and the military, to his resolve and courage, and to the selection of reform-spirited officials. The reforms not only addressed problems of that time, but also had lasting influence that impacted later generations.

In China's modern history, Deng Xiaoping was a master of reform and innovation. He was never a follower of set rules, but a doer who was not affected by his life's ups and downs. He never recoiled from challenges and dangers, but took on the responsibility of pushing the most difficult reforms in China. When the country was debating whether it was going on the socialist or capitalist road, Deng boldly proposed the idea that socialism could also develop a market economy, leading China onto a fast lane to economic transformation. He initiated the great debate on the standards of truth, rehabilitating the wronged and bringing order to the country, once again guiding the CPC and the country back onto the correct track. He was also the chief architect of the "One Country, Two Systems" principle, which prepared the theoretical ground for the return of Hong Kong and Macao. The principle not only enriched and developed Marxism, but also broke the walls of certain concepts to further the building of Chinese socialism. Without his efforts, China would not have entered the socialist market economy so quickly.

The ability to lead and inspire their people to achieve the set goals

People are the main force to push social development, yet they are also the most complicated category in terms of national governance. This is why besides strong will and wisdom, leading figures must also have charisma and outstanding personal qualities. These qualities are mainly reflected in their aspirations, emphasis on national interests, focus on goals, and an inspiring personality. As an ancient Chinese saying goes, "With people's strength mustered, a country becomes invincible; with people's wisdom collected, a country fears no one." The ability to unify the people, to pool strength together for nation building, to safeguard national pride and interests, and to support national development is what differentiates leaders from ordinary people, and is an essential quality for any leadership. Outstanding leading figures generally have higher goals, loftier pursuits, and better self-cultivation. They are the role models for their people for their ability to integrate the power of truth and character, the interests of the country and the people, and the will of the leadership and the people, to create positive energy and a favorable environment.

Leading figures accomplished in governance are all able to exert influence over the people, to muster their strength, to lead their development, and to win their support. It is these traits that made the leaders who they were and helped them consolidate their positions. Some of the best examples are found in modern China. Mao Zedong, a great leader of the Chinese people, lost six family members during the people's liberation, including one of his sons on the battlefield of the Korean War. Zhou Enlai, another senior Chinese leader, was greatly loved by the people for his integrity and character. Taking the lead and setting good examples for the people, he was loyal to the cause of the CPC and his promise to the people. He won the love of the Chinese and the respect of the world, and will be forever remembered as the "son of the Republic."

Besides personal charisma and qualities, leading figures should also have the ability to deliver clear message and lead the people. They must be capable of turning their will into popular goals, and uniting and inspiring the people to fight for these goals. Dr. Martin Luther King touched the hearts of millions of Americans with his "I Have a Dream" speech, sparking the fire of pursuing freedom and equality across America, and creating a new chapter of the non-violent civil rights movement. Likewise, in "Carry the Revolution Through to the End," his New Year's message for 1949, Mao Zedong successfully mobilized the army and the people in gaining the final victory of the Chinese Civil War and liberating all of China.

As stated above, these four essential capacities are central in making great leaders, and grow and extend to new levels as they are integrated with other required capabilities. They can be mimicked but cannot be copied. These capacities could also become the origin of the force to push national and social development through the implementation of leaders' governance strategies and measures. Undeniably, without a platform to apply these qualities, leaders will not be able to show these capacities or be acknowledged by the public. With a proper platform, these qualities will quickly release enormous energy and bring profound changes to a nation and to the world. Early in his tenure, Xi Jinping received such cynical remarks from Western media that "Xi made a point, and we hope what he said can be achieved, but judging from the current situation we are not hopeful." What happened later surprised the world. Within one year's time, Xi reshaped China's governance pattern with unparalleled charisma and ability, and won the recognition and trust from inside and outside the CPC with solid facts of progress. According to the *Washington Post*, an opinion poll conducted in 30 countries around the world showed that Xi was the most popular state leader globally. US President Obama commented on the result that it only took two years for Xi to be so influential in China, which was really impressive. This shift of opinion essentially traces back to the powerful energy that emanates from Xi's leadership capacities, a testimony to the real value of leading figures.

CHAPTER FIVE

Core Capabilities of Xi Jinping's Governance

Key Phrases

- Confidence and strong political will
- Vision and total control
- Tenacity and fearlessness in reform
- Character and charisma to lead the people

The pioneering nature of Chinese socialism and the unique features of China's governing system have determined that the core capabilities of its leaders must answer to the specific needs of China, otherwise it would be very hard to steer such a large country. In addition to the differences of China's political system and its mission, there are two special conditions that ask for higher qualifications from a Chinese leader. First, China still has a weak economic base. China is the world's largest country in terms of population, which is four times that of the USA, almost three times the EU, and 10 times Japan. Unfortunately, China's per capita GDP is only 1/8 that of the USA, and 1/6 that of Japan despite its current status as the world's second largest economy. Second, China still needs to raise the educational level of its citizens. Modernizing China in all sectors and building a strong socialist country demands a higher level of civic qualities, which required that Chinese leaders have more comprehensive and special capabilities. Through comparison and analysis, the ability and judgment Xi showcased in his governance has fully demonstrated the essential capabilities that are required of the leadership of a socialist country, by integrating situations and trends of the world, of China, of the CPC, of society, and of the people. According to the general requirements, there are Chinese elements fusing the common traits and special needs of China. Therefore, the essential capabilities of Xi's governance are more integrated, more inclusive, and more viable, compared with leading abilities in the general sense.

Xi's essential governing capabilities are mainly reflected in his confidence and strong political will, his vision and overall control, his tenacity and fearlessness in reform, and his character and charisma in leading the people. These capabilities have common characteristics with the abilities of leaders, but are not exactly the same and have gone beyond the usual criteria to construct a system of governing abilities. The confidence and strong political will and the character and charisma are "soft abilities," while the vision and overall control, tenacity, and fearlessness in reform are "hard abilities." By fully applying the four essential capabilities, the Chinese leadership has been able to promote the integrated, comprehensive, systemic and efficient progress of the governance of China.

CONFIDENCE AND STRONG POLITICAL WILL

Characteristics
- Strong conviction and lofty goals
- Focusing on the ultimate goal and key areas
- People-oriented approach and national prosperity
- Global vision and strategic planning

Only when leading figures are firm in their convictions can the leadership hold its grounds and uphold principles, and not lose direction, fluctuate, or become scared of risks. Only when leading figures are confident can the leadership itself be resolute and swift in action, and not sway, hesitate, or find it hard to make decisions. In *Lifting Out of Poverty –Talks on Governance*, Xi Jinping wrote, "Only with prior planning can we avoid being misled afterwards." Before making decisions, we should hear the opinions from all sides to understand the issues at hand and find patterns; once a decision is made, it should not be changed before the problem is solved. He also suggested that officials should "not lose their cool in the face of major crises" and "not panic at crucial junctures." It is not hard to see that Xi has always valued the cultivation of strategic composure, emphasizing early planning, avoiding confusion, and ensuring calmness before crises.

Over the past few years, Xi has fully exhibited a strong political conviction and confidence in the governance of China—it is reflected in the clear position on the socialist banner and path, in the resolute attitude on the country's future and the people's well-being, and in the firm conviction of loyalty of communists in front of any turmoil and test. With lofty goals and firm political conviction, he has a keen political sense, is forward-looking and courageous, and has a profound political cultivation. Just as Henry Kissinger commented, Xi conveys a strong will and capabilities with his every move.

Strong conviction and lofty goals

Ideals determine belief, and belief embodies pursuit. Political belief and goals are what make great leaders serve their country and people. Belief in one's goals leads to open-mindedness, tenacity, integrity, diligence, and righteousness. Without beliefs, it would be impossible to embark on great undertakings and lead a nation. Xi, under family influence, developed his convictions about communism early in his life, and gradually became a staunch communist. It is his firm belief that CPC members and leaders cannot have any doubts in their convictions; otherwise the foundation of the Party will be shaken. In his speech at a seminar commemorating the 110th birthday of CPC's veteran leader Chen Yun, Xi stressed that the ideals and convictions of communists are the marrow of their faith. Without, or with weak, ideals or convictions, they would be deprived of their marrow and suffer from the "lack of backbone." He called upon the entire CPC to remain firm in the ideals and convictions of communists, open up their minds to reflect the changes of the world, hold to the correct views on the world, on life, and on their values, and work hard for the common goal of realizing Chinese socialism.

An unswerving communist, Xi is imbued with a lofty character and great ideals, which are assets of all communists who place the ultimate goals above anything else. In the early years of his political career, he pondered two questions: What path to take and what his goals were. He determined that it was not for personal gains or a successful career, but to serve the people and make contributions to the country. Since he became China's top leader, Xi announced that CPC's responsibility was to unify and lead the entire Party and the Chinese people in carrying forward the historic mission of rejuvenating the Chinese nation. It was more than a declaration and it was not an empty promise: it was a solemn promise made by a responsible statesman. He showed great confidence in the path, theories, and system and culture of the country, and the strong conviction of Chinese Communists to continue on China's own path of development.

Since the CPC's 18th National Congress a few years ago, Xi has pushed for reforms and new policies despite many difficulties, fulfilling the mission of a true communist and statesman, and giving the people strength derived from his political convictions and belief. It is because of this strength that he does not fear the obstructions of foreign hostile forces, counters the instigations of those with ulterior motives in China, breaks into the forbidden zone of reform, combats corruption and runs the Party with strict discipline. With his courage to take on responsibilities, Xi has become a role model for the Party and the people.

Focusing on the ultimate goal and key areas

Those who do not have a plan for the whole picture are not capable of planning for a single sector. Leaders with strong political conviction must be strategists with outstanding governing capabilities. Without the support of governing capabilities, deviation will certainly deter the development of the Party and the country. Xi Jinping is a strategist with a holistic view on development. His judgments are based on strategic considerations and a broad vision; he makes decisions with careful thinking, and is good at steering the overall work of the Party and the country, at focusing on the key points of core problems, at disclosing patterns through phenomena, and at seeking pragmatic approaches to solving China's problems. He has always centered his governance practice around practical problems and key problems. The Chinese Dream, Two Centenary Goals, Four-Pronged Comprehensives Strategy, and Five-in-One Development Philosophies are the results of his in-depth thinking and planning, which follow the objective laws and patterns, are based on China's realities, and are pushed forward with coordinated efforts. He has successfully held onto the key problems of development and reform.

First, he has an overall outlook on the governance of China. Xi is thinking deep and wide, and preparing for the future. In the last few years, he has targeted the bottlenecks preventing development and closely centered on the goal of realizing the Chinese Dream. Pushing forward a series of strategic and profound measures for the continued development of China, Xi guaranteed a good start with careful strategic planning.

Second, he has a keen awareness of problems. Xi is good at discovering problems, and at finding the "entry points" to problems. He has the courage to carry out reforms in difficult areas, and employs systemic approaches to deal with individual problems. Every major speech or policy was problem-oriented, and came after careful analysis and with concrete solutions.

Third, he uses research-based methods. Xi has learned from the methods of his predecessors—Mao Zedong's attention to the main problems, his crystal clear exposition of essential points, his foresight, and his grand outlook on the cause of the Party and the state against the backdrop of history and global development, and Deng Xiaoping's global view and strategic thinking that set China's growth in motion by integrating with the world and for the future. Xi pays equal attention to domestic and international issues, to the work of the Party and the country, to pushing reform to new depths in all areas, and to tackling problems in association with the overall situation. He emphasizes driving domestic reform through opening up, actively engaging in global governance and the world economy, developing China by integrating with the world, gaining an objective and clear understanding of China's problems, paying equal attention to developed and less developed areas, to urban areas and rural areas, and to GDP and the quality of life, and ensuring prosperity for all Chinese. The emphasis on research-based methods has enabled Xi to practice the art of governance with a focus on key problems.

People-oriented approach and national prosperity

"The people are the foundation of the state; stability is achieved when the people lead contented lives." Upholding the integration of the people first principle and the pursuit of national prosperity, Xi has always put the people at the heart of all goals, stressing relying on the people to achieve prosperity and achieving prosperity for the people's well-being. After the CPC's 18th National Congress, he summed up his mission as "serving the people and taking on the responsibility." In his governance, President Xi links his own happiness and concerns to those of the people, creating a bond with the people. He makes sure that the most pressing problems of immediate concern to the people are addressed with due consideration and he evaluates the results based on public participation, on letting the people take charge, and on bringing them benefits.

Xi Jinping has always implemented the people first principle with action. When he was working in Ningde, a poverty-stricken area of Fujian Province, he initiated a program to build modern housing for local villagers, who had lived under thatched roofs for generations, and for fishermen who lived in their boats with no houses on land. This was an early attempt to provide the poor with proper housing in China. During his service in Fuzhou City, Xi dealt with pollution from catering services and took action to ensure food security, which was warmly welcomed by the people. He was also among the first secretaries of any provincial CPC committee to offer help to migrant workers. When he was in Zhejiang Province, Xi took active measures to help migrant workers find housing, receive medical care, and ensure their children have school education. Since 2012, Xi has been focusing on integrating the people-oriented approach with pursuing national prosperity and has implemented a series of programs on income distribution, food security, medical care, educational equality, old-age security, and housing, with concrete progress.

Global vision and strategic planning

It is universal that outstanding leaders have a global vision and are capable of dealing with international relations, facilitating global governance, and promoting peaceful development of the world. In this age of economic globalization and the Internet, it is becoming increasingly important to properly handle relations with other countries. Some Western scholars have commented that Xi Jinping's success will affect the futures of China and the world. It is true that in leading China's integration with the world and in building a new world order, Xi has exhibited the wisdom and character of a strategist and the vision and ability of a state leader.

First of all, he has confidence. During his overseas visits, Xi tactfully responded to the malicious attacks on China, by saying, "The world is big, with all kinds of people, and, unsurprisingly, it is very noisy," and "There are all kinds of birds in the cage; if we throw out the noisy ones, the cage would be too silent. We are used to the noise; it's nothing new." Remarks such as these have fully demonstrated his confidence and humor. Next, he shows great sagacity. When tensions arose between the USA and Russia, Xi called upon the world to jump out of the Cold War mentality and the zero-sum game. Responding to doubts about the Chinese Dream, he explained the similarity of the Chinese Dream with the dreams of Europe and the United States, ingeniously answering the questions and drawing closer with countries with similar dreams. Finally, he has generosity. In diplomatic relations, Xi believes in common development and security for all, stressing that China will not only develop its own economy, but will also help others do the same. After some politicians criticized China as a "free rider" in the past 30 years, Xi said when promoting the Belt and Road Initiative, "China is willing to provide opportunities and room for our neighbors for common development. You can take a ride on our express train or just hitchhike. All are welcome." These new thoughts and theories of Xi have jumped out of the traditional diplomatic playbook and the old security outlook of the Cold War era, providing strong positive energy for global peace and development, which presents China as an open, inclusive, and responsible country on the international stage. He has won wide acclaim for China and created a favorable international environment for its development. Today, China is drawing great attention with its every move. A few years ago, "confidence" was the word used by Western media to describe Xi, but today they are referring to him as a "reliable statesman," "a strong, confident and firm epitome of China," and "someone that will change China." As Henry Kissinger said, Xi is setting a new image for China globally.

II. Vision and Total Control

Characteristics
- Good planning and strategic foresight
- Overall planning and focusing on key points
- Rule of law and rule of virtue
- Courage and good judgment

A firm control of the overall situation is a core capacity indispensable for leadership. Without this ability, leaders will not be able to perform their functions and carry out reform, and will easily bring their nations into disorder or collapse. Take the former Soviet Union's disintegration for example, besides Mikhail Gorbachev's "new thoughts" which weakened the political guidance, his lack of overall control was a fatal factor. In contrast, modern-day Russia is regaining its status and ability to maintain stability despite the expansion of NATO and Western sanctions largely because of Putin's firm control. Evidently, the leadership's ability to keep the situation under control determines the fate of their nation.

For many Western scholars, one of Xi Jinping's most outstanding characteristics is his ability to exert overall control. His governance practice has also shown that he has been improving the methods of leadership and improving the ability to take overall control. In an article written in 2004, Xi argued that a good leader knows the art of leadership, by understanding the key points, the approach, the patterns, and the rhythm. In work, according to him, there are three levels of performance. The first level is the highest level, including the awareness of problems and vigilance against problems, the ability to prevent problems before they happen, and the ability to take command with ease. The second level describes officials who work hard, regularly work overtime, and despite the inability to prevent problems from happening, they are able to take measures to address them, i.e., their diligence makes up for it. The third level is the lowest level, referring to officials who are slow to respond and take action, who are unable to spot problems, and unable to solve problems or turn a blind eye to problems.

Rooted in traditional Chinese culture, Xi's governance style has clear characteristics. He focuses more on the overall situation, is more flexible, and at the same time respects China's realities. His focus on key problems and his pragmatic approach have brought about some of the boldest reforms in Chinese history.

Good planning and strategic foresight

Only with a comprehensive understanding of their country's history, current situations, politics, economics, culture, and society can leaders have the confidence to steer national development towards higher ground. Xi Jinping's solid steps of personal growth enabled him to develop an overall understanding of the direction, path, difficulties, and key areas of Party and national governance. With profound understanding and comprehensive knowledge, he is thus more capable of practicing governance to better effect.

First, he has an understanding of the developments of the CPC, the country, and the world. Xi is a man of ideals, goals, and wisdom. Devoted to continuing China's development and solving its problems, he has accumulated rich governance experience in different provinces and cities, which has deepened his understanding of the conditions of the Party, the country, society, and the people, and facilitated his governance of the Party, the state, and the military, and the planning of economic, political, cultural, social, and ecological development. All of these are based on his in-depth understanding of the history and current situation of the Party and the country, and on his comparison and research on the conditions of China and the world, which has enabled him to quickly take total control.

Second, he has developed overall and holistic planning. In managing the CPC and national affairs, Xi has clear goals and plans based on strict logic and research. To begin with, he pushes forward coordinated efforts to govern the Party, the state, and the military with equal intensity, carrying out campaigns against corruption in the Party, pushing systemic reforms in the country, and strengthening the efforts to build a strong army. Next, building a moderately prosperous society in all respects, taking reform to new levels, implementing the rule of law, and strengthening Party discipline have become a strategic plan for the Party and the nation. Lastly, a holistic approach has been taken to seek economic, political, cultural, social, and ecological progress, addressing every problem in state development and governance.

Third, he shows great pragmatism. Xi is a staunch practitioner of Marxism, always proceeding from realities, putting theory into practice, and seeking truth from facts. Not bound by doctrines, never blindly copying from others or following the old path, he believes in action and the people to resolve China's problems based on realities, and opposes vanity projects and fake prosperity. On the matter of economic growth, he questioned the possibility and necessity of maintaining double-digit growth, and came to the conclusion that it was neither necessary nor possible. As China entered the "new normal" with slowed growth, Xi admonished the Party to keep a clear head and be pragmatic in seeking quality and sustainable growth. On the matter of sustainable development of China's economy and society, he stresses gaining a deep understanding of the complete situation and domestic and international trends, holding to the correct direction and heading towards the goals, understanding the opportunities and challenges, taking active measures to expand the advantages, and making systemic planning for future development.

Overall planning and focusing on key points

Overall planning and focusing on key points was a governance strategy in ancient China and has been integrated in the CPC's governance practice. Learning from ancient wisdom, Xi emphasizes strategic and holistic thinking and admonishes against distraction by odds and ends. In national governance, there are two types of problems: core and fundamental problems and general and secondary problems. Since 2012, Xi has put his focus on addressing the main problems that affect the future of the Party and country, personally engaging in the planning and implementation of a series of measures to solve chronic problems at deeper levels. His efforts have brought about coordinated development and progress in the Party, the state, and the military.

Rule of law and rule of virtue

To achieve national revitalization, equal attention should be paid to the rule of law and the rule of virtue. The absence of the rule of law will shake the foundation and without the rule of virtue the country will have no soul. After the CPC's 18th National Congress, Xi has explored a new path of national governance, integrating the rule of law and the rule of virtue and strengthening law enforcement. At the fourth group study session of the Political Bureau of the CPC Central Committee, he pointed out that the Party must integrate the rule of law and the rule of virtue, promote legal progress and ethical progress, and enhance discipline by others and self-discipline. He stressed that without the rule of virtue the nation will lose its foundation and vitality, and without the rule of law the nation will be plunged into a state of chaos. In the past few years, Xi has prioritized the rule of law and also taken concrete measures to implement the rule of virtue. With the promulgation of guiding documents on promoting the rule of law and the continued campaign on cultivating core socialist values, China is striving to practice the rule of law and the rule of virtue side-by-side.

The three main measures are: first, improving the educational level of citizens, inheriting the essence of traditional Chinese culture, enhancing China's soft power, eliminating vulgarity and backwardness in the culture, and developing a positive energy of the Chinese nation; second, strengthening law enforcement, governing the country by the Constitution, by the law, and by regulations, strictly holding to principles and bottom lines, emphasizing the habit of behaving within the boundary of laws and regulations, breaking hidden illegal practices, and ensuring strict law enforcement and discipline; and third, building a team of officials with the conscientiousness to implement the rule of the law and the rule of virtue, improving the governance system and modernizing the governing capacity, realizing interaction between the system and the officials, and ensuring systemic and organizational implementation of the rule of law and the rule of virtue.

Courage and good judgment

Xi's practice of governance has fully showcased his ability to see through the surface of things, to be resolute in decision-making and take quick action, and to address key issues with speed and precision. After the CPC's 18th National Congress, when many were not expecting much, Xi launched a sweeping campaign against corruption. He was resolute and quick in action in the face of this life and death fight. Two months later, former Deputy Secretary of Sichuan Provincial Party Committee Li Chuncheng was removed from office, the first "tiger" to be dealt with in the wake of the 18th National Congress. Subsequently, action was also taken against Zhou Yongkang's underlings in Sichuan, in the petroleum industry, and in politics and the legal system. Facts have proven that the campaign was carried out in accordance with the law and followed strict procedures, reflecting the ability of Xi to crack down on corruption with resolve and courage. Military-related affairs are very sensitive and precaution is a must in dealing with issues inside the military. Fully aware of the harm of corruption in the higher ranks of the army, Xi knew that it was a huge threat to national security and stability if the corrupt officials in the military were not taken down. Making up his mind, Xi left himself no option but to sweep corruption out of the army. The fall of top generals Guo Boxiong and Xu Caihou sent a clear signal to the entire army, addressing their concern and mustering their strength. Cleared of the negative influences, the army regained vitality with a brand new image.

Xi is also a master of handling emergencies. When he was working in Zhejiang Province in 2005, Typhoon Matsa, the biggest in five decades, hit the province hard. Xi had prearranged the evacuation of civilians from construction sites, coasts, and other hazardous areas, transporting 1.24 million people in 20 hours. Only two persons died during the typhoon. It was a miracle compared to what happened in the USA during Hurricane Katrina, which had a death toll of over 1,000 people. In the nine months following Xi's inauguration, a major earthquake hit Sichuan Province and a terrorist attack took place in Xinjiang. Faced with natural disasters and the threat of terror, Xi was quick in response and composed in command, sending relief to the quake center and quickly assuming control of the situation in Xinjiang.

Besides his insight and strong will, Xi is also a pragmatist who despises any form of empty talk. In a 2006 article in the book *Zhijiang Xin Yu*, or *New Visions for Zhejiang Province*, Xi called on officials to be down to earth, admonishing them "not to listen to empty promises, not to believe in superficial skills, not to adopt beautiful but meaningless titles, and not to engage in cheating and dishonesty." When he became China's president, he talked about the perils of empty words and the importance of hard work. In the three guidelines for ethical behavior and the three basic rules of conduct, prudence in exercising power, self-discipline and good faith become the basic political principle for CPC members—a fundamental rule for self-improvement and clean governance. All CPC members have been greatly encouraged by the example of Xi, working hard and taking on responsibilities to address problems. Under the central leadership, they are striving to revitalize China through concrete work.

III. Tenacity and Fearlessness in Reform

Characteristics
- Broad vision and overall innovation
- Bearing responsibilities and duties
- Profound thinking and exploring new paths
- Selflessness, fearlessness, and persistence

"The intelligent man changes with the times; the wise man governs with different approaches under different situations," one of the ancient sayings goes. Reform and creation are the mission of leaders. Reform is central to the rise of a nation and social progress; and pushing reforms relies on the courage and ability of great leaders. For a political party, the transformation from a revolutionary party to a governing party means that it cannot rest on its laurels without change; otherwise it will only lead to a rigid system and even downfall of the regime. That is why the ability to reform and innovate is extremely important for leading figures, which directly determines the sustainability of their countries. Throughout history, it was always reforms that brought in new eras and created prosperity. Mao Zedong, a pioneer of breaking the old and creating the new, not only led the Chinese people to overhaul their nation, but also introduced the most profound social reforms in the history of China, which laid the foundation for a bright future. When China was lagging behind the world, it was Deng Xiaoping who broke the counterproductive rules and got rid of the planned economy, and made science and technology the primary productive forces. The reform and opening-up initiative ushered in a new era of Chinese socialism with unprecedented innovation in the system.

After he took office, Xi Jinping proved himself to be a bold reformer. The new challenges and new goals pressed him to map a greater picture of overall reform at higher levels. Since 2012, striving to promote progress for mankind and to innovate social systems, he has led the Chinese people to launch a great revolution that abandons obsolete mindsets and eliminates all kinds of constraints, exploring a new path of state governance in a socialist country.

Broad vision and overall innovation

An open mind embraces innovation. Xi's way of thinking is open, systemic, and holistic. In a few years' time, he has exhibited openness and overall consideration in reform and innovation. For him there is no forbidden zone, no constraint, and no boundary to the reform. He dares to break the old and establish the new, tackling problems and embracing the world with an open mind. As China opens up its market resources to the world, the country is pushing reform of mixed ownership, speeding up the development of free trade zones, and implementing the Belt and Road Initiative, in order to enhance the quality of an open economy. In driving reform with new thinking, new systems, and new models, there is no blind spot or dead end. The Four-Pronged Comprehensives Strategy is the best example to illustrate Xi's innovative spirit. The Decision of the Third Plenary Session of the CPC 18th Central Committee and the ensuing reform measures have shown that Xi's new thoughts and strategies on governance are being implemented in all areas, including politics, the economy, the military, diplomacy, culture, society, and Party building. It needs to be pointed out that different from other leaders, Xi has multiple reform targets and is skilled at coordinating all areas to achieve overall effectiveness. By practicing modern governance in China, he aims at comprehensive development in this socialist country, reviving and enhancing its national power to prove the superiority of socialism and the system's advanced nature in human progress. The new generation of CPC leadership, elected at its 18th National Congress, has been embarking on overall reform at new depths, solving long-standing and intertwined problems under effective top-level design, bringing the benefits of reform to all sectors, and distributing the dividends of the reform to the people. We have reason to believe that as the reform furthers, China will undoubtedly open a new chapter on this new starting point towards a better future.

Bearing responsibilities and duties

It is their historic mission that requires Chinese Communists to take on responsibilities with courage. For some time, there have been officials who choose to muddle along and stay away from trouble, failing to perform their duties or shouldering their responsibilities. This negative trend has seriously undermined the Party's cause, polluted society, and harmed the image of the CPC and the government.

Xi Jinping knows how much damage this could do to the CPC and the country. Great risks lie ahead when China is in a crucial stage of development and in pursuit of the Chinese Dream. All CPC members must take on their responsibilities and work hard for a better China, and all leading officials must boldly take action to reform and innovate. Efforts must be made in terms of the policy and mechanisms to encourage those who dare to try and take the lead, so that the entire CPC will embrace a healthy culture of industriousness and a sense of duty.

Since 2012, "responsibility" has become a frequent term in Xi's speeches, "We must take due responsibilities," "Party members must perform their duties, and must not avoid responsibilities or lie to the organization," "Dare to take responsibilities and stick to principles in front of major issues," "When the young have ideals and take on responsibilities, there is hope for the nation and the people." These remarks, as plain as they are, showcase Xi's courage to take responsibilities for the nation, and reveal how doing so could affect China's future.

In the last few years, he has been enriching and expanding the contents of responsibilities, putting the rejuvenation of China at the forefront. In the management of officials, the courage to take on responsibilities has become one important criterion, which determines how far an official could go on the career ladder. Those who think independently, take concrete action, perform their duties, and hold onto the principles will be promoted. Rigid assessment criteria for officials have been abolished, and performance in the face of major, difficult issues has become a new factor in laying down the correct track for officials' advancement. Practicing what he preaches, Xi sets a role model for all Party members and officials by upholding his duties of office, putting people's interests first, and shouldering responsibilities.

On matters of national sovereignty, he does not waver or hesitate, but holds firm to principles on such matters as the Diaoyu Islands, the South China Sea, and the Taiwan question, telling the world the position of the Chinese and making his people proud. On matters of life and death, he upholds the banner against corruption, and announced war on all interest groups, ensuring everyone is equal in the eyes of the law, and wholeheartedly devoting himself to the causes of the nation, which greatly inspired the people. On matters or challenges that may affect the country's future, he is resolute in furthering reforms, without fear of risks or consequences. His courage and wisdom are fully reflected in the way forward, despite great difficulties, and his spirit and perseverance in pushing forward reform have earned him the utmost respect from the people.

Profound thinking and exploring new paths

Historically, accomplished reformers fall into two categories: those who begin with small things and grow stronger step by step, and those who make plans with overall consideration and achieve coordinated development. As a modern reformer, Xi integrates the two approaches, applying their advantages in practice. On the one hand, there are grand goals and plans such as the Two Centenary Goals, the Chinese Dream, the Five-in-One Development Strategy, and Four-Pronged Comprehensives Strategy, and the Belt and Road Initiative. On the other hand, there are the full implementation of further reform measures, the resolve to streamline the administration and delegate powers to lower levels, the precision strike on corruption, the clear standards for good officials, and the detailed plans to boost China's national football sport. Xi has set a perfect example for integrating overall planning and concrete implementation.

Xi has an open mind for new things with a pioneering spirit and the boldness to explore new possibilities. This is best exhibited in his remark, "A great cause always faces more challenges, which requires us to explore and innovate." Since 2012, leading the Chinese on the path of socialism, Xi has been making headway in innovating his theories and practice on governance. Putting innovation at the center of national strategies, he introduced systemic reforms in the superstructure, the economic base, and the productive relations. On national governance, he is striving to modernize the governance system and the governing capacity, putting equal emphasis on the reform and opening up, and on the rule of law. In international relations, he proposed new types of diplomacy based on China's role, developing relations with both the major powers and neighboring countries, and taking a more active role in international affairs. In economic development, he stresses the equally important roles of the market and the government, emphasizing development quality and efficiency rather than the GDP-driven growth, in the pursuit of a healthy and sustainable path. In military development, he stresses building the army with strong convictions and advanced technology, pushing reforms in national defense, and ensuring the army's combat readiness. On SOE development, he upholds public ownership as the basic economic system, putting efforts into innovating the internal mechanism, overcoming institutional flaws, and improving the efficiency of SOEs, and pioneering a new road to enhance the essential capacity of the state-owned economy. All of Xi's efforts will definitely power China to take a leading role in development in the long run.

Selflessness, fearlessness, and persistence

Great leaders all have the ability to proceed despite interference, the ability to remain calm in front of dangers and difficulties, and such qualities as integrity, straightforwardness, honesty, generosity, and strong willpower. They are fearless in seeking national development, wholeheartedly devoted to the well-being of their people, and persevere in their pursuit of lofty goals. They have great ideas to revitalize their countries, and make every effort to realize these goals, ignoring personal gain and not fearing sacrifice when there is a need. These qualities of leading figures are powerful and radiant, sometimes having direct bearing on their countries' direction and future. In the history of the CPC, Mao Zedong, Deng Xiaoping and other great leaders all exemplified these qualities, as does Xi now.

As known to all, currently China is facing great difficulties and challenges, and the CPC's new generation of leadership has thus taken on huge responsibilities. On the one hand, existing problems are resurfacing during the country's development; on the other, new problems keep arising. Without a strong leader of great will and integrity, there will be no guarantee on the path of Chinese socialism, the comprehensive reforms, the transformation of the growth model, the fight against corruption, and the campaign to eradicate poverty. Failure to carry out these missions would lead to failure of the system. In the past few years, Xi has gone to great lengths to reassure the Party and the people of China's bright future. In front of growing ideological disturbances, he holds fast to Chinese socialism, boosting confidence in China's path. As the reforms enter a crucial stage, he is resolute in pushing forward reform plans, not yielding to pressure. When negative opinions began to doubt the strength of the fight against corruption, he responded with more rigorous action and continued to sweep corrupt elements out of the Party. In the face of the difficulties in the economy, amidst misunderstandings and attacks, he kept pressing forward with reforms to the economic structure, emphasizing the necessity to undergo "labor pains" for future gains. When some complained that the poverty eradication goal was impossible to achieve, he reiterated that the CPC will not leave anyone behind and rearranged the schedules with more detailed plans. Xi's willpower and charisma has uprooted any doubt about China's development, and brought the people great courage and strength.

IV. Character and Charisma to Lead the People

Characteristics
- Self-cultivation and devotion to the nation
- Unity of knowing and doing and leading by example
- Care for the people which nurtures synergy of the entire nation
- Inclusiveness and generosity which win respect from far and near

"A Mandela type of politician," "a wise man," "an outstanding leader for China," "a leader of similar qualities with Mao Zedong and Deng Xiaoping," "a leader with unprecedented capacity," "a new geopolitical master"—all these were comments on Xi from leaders, a genuine depiction of his excellent qualities. A few years of governance practice has established his personal style as an amiable, practical, and firm leader on the international political stage. His global vision, focus on progress, and pioneering spirit show the world what the leader of a rising country is like.

Self-cultivation and devotion to the nation

"The ancients, who wished to promote illustrious virtue under heaven, first had to rule their own states well. Wishing to govern their states well, they first had to manage their fiefdoms well. Wishing to manage their fiefdoms well, they first had to cultivate themselves." In China, education and self-cultivation are always valued, especially for officials. Xi knows well that to promote civility in the country and to build an advanced Party, education must come first. As the leader of China, one must "rectify their heart, and seek to be sincere in their thoughts." To do this, a good education, resourcefulness and knowledge, profound thinking and wisdom are some of the preconditions. Leaders must cultivate themselves before governing their countries, and strive to practice governance with knowledge, wisdom, and character.

In self-cultivation, Xi exhibits these following characteristics:

First, he shows conscientiousness. From childhood Xi took a liking to reading and developed good learning habits. He carried this habit to office, seeing it as a responsibility and a conscientious pursuit. For decades, Xi has always been an avid learner, and regardless of his position in office and the burden of work, he keeps reading and learning new things. He believes that only through learning can one progress, and that learning and reading will help one work better. After the CPC convened its 18th National Congress, he chaired group learning sessions to encourage the entire CPC to read books and improve their knowledge of the Party's theories. Under his leadership, the CPC is focusing more on studying and research and the positive influence has reached the people.

Second, he has incredible resourcefulness. Xi reads extensively and absorbs knowledge from all areas. By studying Marxism-Leninism, Mao Zedong Thought, and the theories of Chinese socialism, he is able to enhance his leading capabilities with the correct theories and methods to be applied in practice. By studying topics such as strategy, politics, philosophy, economics, history, sociology, law, military science, and diplomacy, he is able to expand his knowledge, improve capabilities, and accumulate information for further growth. It is not hard to notice that in both formal and impromptu speeches, he appears to be at ease citing historical references and classics, and his governance strategies have clear signs of integrated knowledge from all schools of thought and a wide variety of sources.

Third, he focuses on practice. Xi has always guided his studies with practice, applying theories in practice, and enhancing his work through learning. After becoming China's president, he put even more emphasis on the purpose of studies, i.e., to solve China's problems and guide its development. The contents of the group study sessions of the CPC Political Bureau have shown that Xi attaches great importance to studying, so that Party officials are capable of solving both pressing problems and deeper-level problems with a sound theoretical foundation, practical knowledge, and competence and governing capacity.

Fourth, he is committed to the teaching of traditional culture. Xi highly values China's traditional culture, calling it the "spiritual home of all Chinese, the wisdom shared by mankind, and the most profound soft power of China." He said, "Only by remembering our roots can we head to a better future; only by carrying forward the tradition can we innovate." Drawing from the essence of traditional Chinese culture, he has given new meaning to benevolence, the people-oriented philosophy, integrity, justice, harmony, and unity, creatively incorporating traditional culture into his governance system. Once again from his articles and speeches, it can be seen that Xi reads extensively, from ancient classics to writings of all schools of thought, and the subjects include economics, politics, society, culture, law, and ethics. Nonetheless, he pays special attention to select only the good parts of ancient wisdom and reevaluates them based on China's realities today to ensure the application of traditional culture goes in line with the requirements of the times.

Unity of knowing and doing and leading by example

An ancient saying goes, "Governance is about righteousness. If you lead the righteous way, who dares to deviate?" The integrity and righteousness of a leader have the power to draw people together and win their support. Image is an important factor in governance. Xi knows that to lead 1.3 billion Chinese, he must be both a strong leader and a man of noble character, and set good examples for the Party and the people in building China with one heart.

Striving to set a good image, Xi believes in self-regulation before regulating the action of others. In office, he has always practiced self-discipline, setting examples for Party members and winning the people's support with integrity and character. First, he is a doer. Xi believes that there is no use in empty talks, and one must take action if they want to achieve anything. Believing that no one is entitled to privileges regardless of their official ranks, he has never made exceptions on this principle, strictly executing the regulations he made. To carry out the Eight Regulations, Xi takes the lead in its implementation, taking only the necessary personnel during visits, avoiding disrupting public traffic, banning welcome slogans and fanfare where he visits, and taking humble accommodation and catering during travels. Second, he leads by example. In implementing policies and measures and in governing the Party with strict discipline, Xi has set good examples for the entire Party with action. At a Political Bureau meeting in 2016, he asked the entire Party to strengthen the conscientiousness of political convictions, overall planning, and learning from the Central Committee and the Political Bureau. He has also pledged to strictly regulate himself, his family, and his deputies. Third, he keeps his word. Xi believes that the authority of a leader comes from his honesty and credibility, and failure to keep one's word and honor one's promise will only cause one to be abandoned by the people. He has always honored his promises to the people, which is one of his most important principles. By furthering the reform and improving people's well-being, he has honored his promise to revitalize China and bring prosperity to the people; by sending aid and investment to countries in need, he has honored his promise to the international community that China is a responsible country; by keeping personal promises to friends and family, he has honored his integrity as a man. It is the honesty, trustworthiness, and other noble aspects of his character that have defined his respectable qualities.

Care for the people which nurtures synergy of the entire nation

The support and love of the people have created a natural bond between Xi and the Chinese people. *The New York Times* carried an article that commented that the Chinese media showed President Xi's casual side—appearing in cartoons, online songs, and most surprisingly, in a steamed dumpling shop. "Xi Dada" (Papa Xi), as the people called him, has created an amiable image more than ever. In one comment, Deutsche Welle said that no Westerner had seen any leader so close with his people. From the day he entered office, Xi set his mission as leading the people towards better lives. After he became China's president, he continued to put people first and took concrete action to fulfill his pledges to the people, who are like family to him.

Since 2012, Xi has publicly expressed his deep love to the people on various occasions. "I shall work day and night to serve the people and the country;" "I will always be of one heart with the people, share happiness and woe with them, and work together with them;" "I will remember the people's trust, and remember my responsibility;"—all of these quotes exemplify Xi's love for the people. On TV, it is easy to notice that when Xi interacts with the people, he is sincere, natural and always at ease. When he ventured in deep snow to a poverty-stricken area in Hebei Province, when he visited migrant workers on construction sites, his amity and genuine care for the people was deeply felt, and as a "man of the people" he has become the center of all Chinese in their pursuit of the Chinese Dream.

Inclusiveness and generosity which win respect from far and near

Such qualities of leading figures as inclusiveness, magnanimity, and generosity can attract support and muster people's strengths. Xi is a master at uniting people, and has unique understandings in this regard. He believes that the key lies in magnanimity and inclusiveness. As a member of the CPC and a national leader, he pays special attention to winning the support of various sectors and mobilizing positive elements in order to achieve progress. In the central leadership, he stresses coordinating the relationships between the "fingers" and the "fist," pointing out "Unity leads to success in work," and "Solidarity is an art, which produces cohesiveness, combat effectiveness, productive forces, and good officials." On ethnic affairs, he emphasizes the common roots and mutual help of China's various ethnic groups, who share a common destiny. On relations with China's Hong Kong, Macao, and Taiwan, he calls for a brotherly bond in jointly realizing the Chinese Dream. On international cooperation, he says, "Strength is not shown in the muscle, but in unity." On China's relations with major powers and neighboring countries, he especially stresses mutual benefit, and the promotion of a multi-polar pattern through harmonious, sincere, and reciprocal cooperation. The open embrace of China towards those with the same goals and those with differences has established a new image of China and of Xi—one of confidence, honesty, pragmatism, inclusiveness, and credibility. His efforts have won wide respect and support, and greatly boosted China's influence.

In conclusion, the four core capabilities, i.e., self-cultivation and devotion to the nation, unity of knowing and doing and leading by example, care for the people and public support, and inclusiveness and good neighborly relations, embody the necessary qualities for the leaders of China, as exemplified in their political convictions and beliefs, the ability to lead and innovate, the courage to take on responsibilities, the love for the nation and the people, and personal qualities. Under an inherent logic, the four capabilities play different roles: The confidence and convictions lead the way in national governance; overall control plays a central role in promoting governance; innovation and creativity bring governance to higher levels; and the personal qualities of leadership boost national image and ensure ultimate success. Supporting and complementing each other, the four capabilities provide powerful support to the development of governance strategies, to their implementation, to strengthening the authority of the central leadership, and to future successes of China's governance practice.

CHAPTER SIX

Development of Xi Jinping's Governance Capabilities

Key Phrases

- Family tradition and positive upbringing
- Hardship and ties with the people
- Rich work experience and leading abilities
- Learning and self-improvement
- Party convictions and leadership

Core capabilities, integrating hard and soft powers, cannot be duplicated or acquired at will. One must go to great lengths and overcome countless difficulties and challenges to obtain them. The cultivation of core capabilities is also related to personal growth, ideals and ambitions, and personal qualities and aptitude. In President Xi's case, it is the result of positive family tradition, trials of hardships, rich practical experience, continuous learning, and a deep faith in the CPC's mission. It is also the response to new developments, the Chinese Dream and the people's wishes, which jointly strengthened these abilities.

I. Family Tradition and Positive Upbringing

Influences

- Character
- Self-cultivation
- Conduct
- Convictions
- Politics

Our parents are our first teachers, and our family is the first school and the cradle of our personality. Family has a vital bearing on our personality, goals and ambitions, and the way we deal with things. Xi Jinping was born to a family of revolutionaries, which undoubtedly prepared him for future growth and a career in the CPC. It must be acknowledged that, however, family background was not everything. It needs to be enhanced with the virtues of traditional Chinese culture and positive conduct of the Chinese Communists. Only in this way can one carry on the traditions of the CPC and contribute to China's development.

Xi grew up in such a family. His father, Xi Zhongxun, joined the CPC at the age of 15 and became the chairman of the Shaanxi-Gansu Soviet government at 21. He was one of the founding members of the PRC and a member of its leadership. During times of war and socialist construction, Xi Zhongxun enjoyed a great reputation in China. Mao compared him to Zhuge Liang, a great strategist and statesman known for his wisdom in Chinese history 2,000 years ago, and a "completely reliable" colleague. Deng Xiaoping spoke highly of him as the person who took risks in his place and pioneered the reform and opening-up drive. Xi's mother, Qi Xin, joined the revolutionary cause when she was 13 years old, followed the Party's leadership her entire life, and was a principled and tenacious communist with deep convictions in the CPC's mission.

Influenced by his parents, Xi Jinping developed a fine character from a young age and his qualities only became stronger as time went by. Like he said, he learned five things from his father: self-cultivation, devotion to work, belief and commitment, patriotism, and simple living. Tracing his footsteps, we can see that Xi Jinping received positive influences early on in life while developing his own personality and qualities.

First, his father had positve influence on his character. Throughout his life, Xi Zhongxun exhibited personal integrity, honesty, and loyalty to the Party, stood firmly against evil, always spoke his mind, and never withdrew from his duties for personal gain or to avoid personal loss. He was a fighter who was seeking truth, and a great man. From childhood, Xi Jinping learned from his father's example, drawing from him the strength of character, looking up to his standards, and fully inheriting his merits and his sense of integrity. After he entered office, Xi exhibited the qualities of his father in his loyalty to the Party, pursuit of truth, upholding of principles, integrity and righteousness.

Second, his father influenced him in self-cultivation. Xi Zhongxun set a positive example at integrating the political character of Chinese Communists with traditional Chinese virtues, living a simple life despite his high office, and forbidding all forms of privilege for himself and his family. He showed his love for his children through discipline, teaching them the importance of self-reliance and hard work, and admonishing against excessive privileges. The strict upbringing of Xi Jinping made him a disciplined, hardworking, and industrious young man, which nurtured him to be a practical, disciplined, and righteous official later in his life.

Third, his father influenced his conduct. Xi Zhongxun, a humble and responsible revolutionary who never sought fame or fortune, or grew arrogant because of his contributions, deeply influenced his son's life and work. At work, Xi Jinping set his mind to doing concrete tasks, leading his colleagues to fight the hardest battles, which was largely attributed to his father's prag-matic role model.

Fourth, he influenced his convictions. Again, his father, Xi Zhongxun led a legendary life of glory and hardship. For 16 years, he suffered immensely from unjust treatment and perse-cution, but still kept to his faith in communism. The father's unwavering convictions in ideals despite difficulties had great impact on his son Xi Jinping who, from a young age, set goals to pursue and formed a tenacious personality in defiance of life's hardships. These had all helped Xi develop an iron will and the ability to stay calm and confident despite difficulties.

Fifth, his father influenced his political views. In times of war and during national construction, Xi Zhongxun exhibited such qualities of good judgment, keeping to the correct direc-tion, and discernment, and an aptitude for maintaining over-all control, promoting solidarity, and addressing tough issues. Learning from his father, Xi Jinping gained valuable knowledge of political wisdom and leadership, which contributed to the development of his governing capabilities.

II. Hardship and Ties with the People

Stages of understanding the people

- Hardship in childhood
- Hardship in youth
- Hardship in the grassroots office

Xi Jinping has always performed his duties of office for the people, planning for their well-being, fighting for their benefit and believing that the CPC must work for the people. Looking back, his deep ties with the people came from his experience in childhood, as a young man, and in the various grassroots posts he held.

First, the hardships in childhood drew him closer to the people. When he was six, his father was removed from office and slandered as an "anti-Party conspirator." Three years later, his father suffered persecution, and his mother was sent to work at a reeducation school for seven years. Forced to separate from his family, Xi suffered immeasurably as a child. He was publicly denounced, starved, exiled, and even detained. Life dealt many heavy blows to him. In the darkest of times, it was the help and care of everyday people that gave him the courage to continue. He was deeply touched and thus formed a natural and genuine bond with the common people. This experience laid the foundation of his people-oriented views after he took office. When he chatted with villagers sitting at their brick beds in the remote mountains, when he brought food to an elderly man, when he kissed the children in a relief tent after an earthquake, it all showed his deep connection to the people, which came naturally for him.

Second, his hardships in youth consolidated his bond with the people. As a child, Xi received help and care from kind people, to whom he was grateful. When he turned 15 and was sent to a rural area in northern Shaanxi, his interaction with the people there developed into a deep bond that proved unbreakable. During his seven years in Shaanxi, he endured all the hardships of the people there: sleeping on earthen beds in cave houses, surviving on corn, and living among fleas. The villagers helped him through; building dams, carrying dung, reclaiming waste land, building roads, and transporting heavy goods in the mountains. His fellow workers taught him about endurance; when his application to join the CPC was rejected many times, it was the common folk who helped him. All these tied Xi closely to the people and the bond grew deeper day by day. The seven-year experience was a vital period for him. Before he went to Shaanxi, the people were more like a helping hand in need, or a hot bowl of soup on a cold night. When he left Shaanxi, the people became close colleagues he could work with, the support he could rely upon, the great friends he could share his thoughts with, and the blood brothers to go through weal and woe together. Such is the reason why Xi has his roots in the people, and why his bond with the people is unbreakable. He said, "When I came here at 15 years old, I was a confused child not knowing where to go; when I left here seven years later, I had clear goals and was full of confidence. I am a man of the people; I have my roots in the Loess Plateau, because it nurtured my ideal: to work for the people." These few lines truthfully depict Xi's deep love for the people.

Third, the hardships of grassroots work deepened his understanding of the people. In January 1974, Xi Jinping's tenth application to join the CPC was accepted and he was soon elected the secretary of his village's CPC branch. He spent one year at the post before going to university. Despite the short time, the experience catalyzed his understanding of the people. When his father was yet to be rehabilitated, the local Party organization took a great risk in accepting him into the CPC and making him the secretary of the village Party branch, a decision based on the people's judgment. Xi was deeply moved by the people's support and their integrity and honesty. As a young man who had no family there, he gained the trust and support of the villagers during his time as a Party secretary. Fully trusting and relying on the people, he led them to build methane heating systems and expand farmland areas, further deepening his understanding of the people, and discovering that true wisdom, justice, and strength lie within the people. Just as Xi said, the life in the villages of Shaanxi opened his eyes to the strength of the people and its source, to the real countryside of China, to the concerns of the people, and to the realities of the country. There is no doubt that his time at the grassroots office laid a solid foundation for the development of his people-centric approach.

The nurturing, love, and support of the people in hardships and adversity formed a natural bond between Xi and the people. It drew him closer to the people, confirmed his convictions to serve the people, and set the tone for his practice of the Party's principles. Putting the people's interests above anything else has become a beacon to guide the entire Party.

III. Rich Work Experience and Leadership Abilities

Stages of development

- The beginning stage
- The growth stage
- The maturing stage

Governing abilities are closely related to work experience. The long history, vast territory, huge population, diverse ethnicities, and unique political system of China necessitate that the leadership understand the country's real situation and the people, and have the ability to make overall planning, top-level design, and systemic and coordinated strategies. These abilities must come from rich work experiences at different levels of work and in different areas.

Compared to other Chinese leaders, Xi worked at more posts in different sectors and at different levels. Starting at the grassroots level in a village Party branch, he served, successively, as the head of counties, prefectures, provincial capitals, coastal provinces, and a municipality directly under the central government. Upon entering the national leadership, he served as secretary of the Secretariat, before being elected as the general secretary of the CPC Central Committee. Xi's office covered all areas, including the Party, government, and the military, with work experience in city and provincial level governments. His rich work experience can be divided into three stages.

The first part of Xi's development began in a northern Shaanxi village in Zhengding County. During his seven years in northern Shaanxi Province, especially during the year he served as the secretary of the local village Party branch, Xi gained first-hand experience with agriculture-related matters, developed a deep understanding of the people, set the goals for his lifetime pursuits, and made up his mind to serve the people, which set the early tone for developing his governing abilities. During his time at Tsinghua University, Xi acquired the necessary knowledge in terms of theories, the way of thinking, and the ability to research, honed his skills of reasoning and judgment, and confirmed his goals and ideals in governing the country, which laid the theoretical basis for developing his governing abilities. Upon graduation, he joined the military where he learned more about military affairs, the army, and the soldiers, broadened his horizons, enhanced his governing and leadership capabilities, and forged his iron will, which prepared him for national governance. Xi formally began his official career at Zhengding County, Hebei Province. There he began to develop the essential abilities of leadership.

At Zhengding, Xi began to explore a path of governance starting with local management. This was reflected in two aspects. First, when making decisions and plans, instead of restricting them to the county, he linked local development with national growth. Second, as a young, capable leader he brought a breath of fresh air to the local government, developing new ideas of governance by addressing key problems and curbing bad tendencies. During his three years at Zhengding, Xi carried out rural reforms and took measures to improve the people's well-being and officials' conduct, beginning to test his approach to dealing with China's problems. This was a prelude to the all-around reforms and strengthening of Party discipline he pushed after entering the national leadership. After he became China's president, Xi put forth the Eight Regulations, which was based on the "six regulations" he proposed in Zhengding 29 years before. The main points included focus on overall planning, avoiding bureaucratic thought, consolidating unified leadership, and leading by example. From the "six regulations" to the

Eight Regulations, from a CPC's county committee to its Political Bureau, Xi continued to practice his governance strategies with coherence and industriousness.

The second growth stage for Xi started in Fujian. For Xi, the 17 years in Fujian Province was a valuable opportunity to hone his leadership skills and develop his leadership abilities. By handling economic, political, and social affairs, and dealing with cross-Straits relations and improving people's livelihood, he entered a crucial stage of growth. In Xiamen, the frontline of China's reform and opening-up drive and cross-Straits relations, he developed an open attitude towards new things, and gained experience dealing with sensitive cross-Straits problems. In Ningde, a poverty-stricken area in Fujian Province, he furthered his understanding of China's realities, began to search for poverty reduction remedies, and tested his theory of the "key minority" in governing officials. In Fuzhou, the capital city of Fujian Province, he enhanced his capacity to govern modern cities and to make overall planning and coordinate all sides. At the Fujian Provincial Government, he furthered his thinking on modern governance and the transformation of government functions, and improved his ability to balance political, economic, and cultural development. In Zhejiang Province, he grew faster in terms of leadership abilities and achieved more on a broader platform. During the five years in Zhejiang, Xi developed his personal style of governance. By exploring new growth models, stimulating market vitality, promoting social impetus for development, solving deeply-rooted problems in accordance with the law, and protecting the environment, he brought the province to higher levels of reform and turned it into an experiment in sustainable development, while improving his abilities to lead economic, social and overall reforms. In Shanghai, despite the short term there, he further enhanced his leadership abilities in this city known as the frontline of China's reform, the vantage point of personnel and resources, and the center of China's economy. Through the platforms of finance, trade, and cooperation, Xi improved his abilities in international cooperation and economic globalization, entering a new stage of development.

From the poorest areas in China to coastal cities and the nation's economic hub, put in different environments and challenged by different problems, Xi had the chance to seek diverse angles to address problems, and opportunities to obtain first-hand experience with China's realities, of its society and its people. These pushed him to become more capable at addressing complicated issues to ensure overall growth. In the 200 essays he wrote, we could clearly see his growth track: from punishing 2,000 officials for their involvement in unauthorized housing projects in Ningde to running the Party and officials with strict discipline, from promoting "limited government" in Zhejiang to transforming government functions, from the "Chenqiao experience" to today's social reforms, from equal emphasis on growth and environment to building a beautiful China, from Shanghai's "four key words" of speed, structure, quality, and benefit to the Five-in-One Development Philosophies of innovation, coordination, green development, opening-up, and sharing of benefits. Xi's growth in this stage was vital to forming his ability to lead.

The third and final maturing stage was after becoming a member of the national leadership. As a member of the Standing Committee of the Political Bureau of the CPC Central Committee in 2007, Xi achieved a major breakthrough in his career. Standing on a higher platform, he had the opportunity to further broaden his horizons, set greater goals, and consolidate his ideals and convictions. By directly participating in the development of Party and state policies, he furthered his understanding of the overall situation of the work, of the Party, and state, and of the intrinsic patterns of Party and national governance. By directly participating in the implementation of decisions and plans, he furthered his understanding of the key links in implementation and enhanced his executing ability. By directly participating in the handling of emergencies and incidents, he further gained strategic composure and improved his ability to keep things under control. To shore up his experience with diplomatic work, Xi visited 40 countries and regions in five years' time enriching his diplomatic experience, hardening his skills of dealing with international relations, and developing his own thinking on diplomacy. Thus, Xi became a comprehensive leader with work experience in all areas and confidently stepped up as the core of China's new generation of leadership.

Looking back, Xi's career, spanning decades of work experience at various posts, laid a solid foundation in practicing governance, fully preparing him in terms of the required theories, strategic thinking, vision and mission, and leadership skills. All these had predetermined his success as China's leader, who exerted enormous influence over the country's development.

IV. LEARNING AND SELF-IMPROVEMENT

Goals
- Learning to enhance education
- Learning to deepen insight
- Learning to apply theories into practice

Theories are the commanding core, the soul, and the source of governance capabilities. It will not be possible to solve China's problems without theoretical guidance. It is evident that Xi's growth not only enriched his work experience, but also helped him develop his own theoretical system. The expanding and improving system has enabled him to fulfill his duties of governance in a more rigorous way.

First, he learned to enhance educational levels. One's education determines his or her performance and potential. Xi has always been an avid learner. He reads extensively and studies conscientiously. During his time in Shaanxi, his greatest treasure was the trunk of books he brought with him and the happiest moments were when he was reading them late at night after work. He has kept that positive habit of reading, and never ceased to accquire new knowledge with an open mind. As he carried more responsibility and worked at higher positions, he further emphasized the importance of learning, because only through learning can we carry on China's history, achieve personal growth, consolidate the Party's governance, and realize national prosperity. He read extensively, covering areas such as history, ancient classics, Marxism-Leninism, politics, military, philosophy, law, and Chinese and foreign literature. His thirst for knowledge and resourcefulness have become two of his most outstanding traits. A positive education not only has supported the development of Xi's abilities and capacities, but also facilitated the development of his theoretical system, enhancing his skills of summarizing, cognition, and the ability to look into the future and uncover the nature of matters. After 2012, each time Xi made a speech, he exhibited the ability to cite classics and historical writings, as well as modern treatises, on literature, history, natural science, etc., with depth and focus. Each important speech is a feast to the mind, fully showcasing the education and acumen of a great leader. There is no doubt that these qualities are a result of hard work and perseverance in learning.

Second, he learned to deepen his insight. Knowledge and insight come in pairs. Without comprehension and insight, knowledge floats on the surface, rendering it useless in forming theories and tackling real problems. President Xi pays special attention to integrating learning, thinking, and practice. First, he incorporates his own understanding into the learning process, in order to crack difficult issues and have effective overall control. Second, he summarizes and categorizes the learned knowledge, and, through questions and criticism, opens up his mind, breaks restrictions, and sets patterns to become a powerful thinker with holistic and integrated thinking. Third, he follows practice with thinking and applies thinking into practice to enhance his governing methods and abilities. In learning and understanding, Xi is skillful at categorizing different views, linking them together, and developing them to new levels. He has the habit of summarizing what he has learned into logic and reasoning, and then into theoretical systems. Since 2012, he has formed his own governance philosophies based on his predecessors' work, by way of keeping the useful ones and abandoning outdated contents.

Third, he learned to apply theories into practice. Knowledge and practice are the two faces of realizing and transforming the world, with knowledge as the base and practice the key. Xi has always upheld the unity of knowing and doing, emphasizing practice instead of empty talk, and is skillful at applying theories into practice. To begin with, he applies knowledge in practice, in work and life and in everyday governance, to prevent blindness in decision-making. Next, he tests theories in practice, hones analytical skills, and enhances his ability to summarize laws and patterns. Lastly, he enhances practice and learning to achieve the unity of knowing and doing, and never stops to consolidate his theoretical knowledge, furthering practice, and expanding ways of thinking to strengthen both thinking and action. Since 2012, Xi has been carrying out reforms in sweeping motion, cracking difficult issues one by one, and breaking new ground with his governance practice. These successes were largely attributed to the unity of knowledge and practice and attention to theoretical studies.

The Book of Rites says: "Learn broadly, examine closely, reflect carefully, discriminate clearly, and practice earnestly." Drawing inspiration from ancient wisdom, Xi has developed a profound culture and knowledge base, a solid theoretical foundation, dialectical thinking, and a rich experience in practice. He has grown and achieved successes through the cycles of learning, thinking, and practicing, which serve as key logic links in his system of thought.

V. Party Convictions and Leadership

Key Phrases
- Determination and loyalty to the Party
- Self-improvement and Party convictions
- Taking on responsibilities and setting a role model

Firm convictions in the Party's pursuit are what distinguish Chinese leaders from leaders of other countries and the source of the energy and vitality of the CPC's cause. This is determined by the fact that the CPC is the only governing party in China. Without firm convictions in the Party's ideals, Party leaders cannot represent the pioneering spirit of the CPC members, nor will they gain the support of the people. History has proven that Party leaders with strong convictions will not only have a strong basis in self-cultivation and improvement, but will also exercise strong leadership over the Party to ensure its long-lasting vitality. Since its 18th National Congress, headed by Xi Jinping, the CPC leadership further strengthened the Party's central role in leading China's development, striving to push forward reforms in politics, economy, society, and culture, and making headway in running the Party and officials with strict discipline. New achievements have been made in the building of Chinese socialism and the Party and the people have never been so united. The CPC has greatly improved its image, exhibiting strong convictions in its ideals, tireless pursuit of its goals, an iron will, and leadership abilities. Like building a skyscraper, leadership abilities do not come in only one day, but are the result of decades of loyalty, convictions, hard work, and pursuit of ideals.

First, CPC leaders need determination and loyalty to the Party. Loyalty to the Party is a precondition and primary requirement for all CPC members. It is the cornerstone for the entire Party. Though he did not personally experience war and revolution before the PRC, Xi is a firm fighter for communism and his loyalty to the Party is pure, selfless, and undoubted. To begin with, his motive to join the Party was pure. Early in life, Xi made up his mind to follow the Party and serve his country as a member of the CPC. His ten applications to join the Party testified to the purity of his motive and his loyalty. Secondly, he is loyal and devoted to the Party. After joining the CPC, Xi has always upheld the Party Constitution and discipline, working hard to improve himself, wholeheartedly following the Party's leadership, and devoting himself to the Party's cause. Decades of commitment and hard work have left concrete marks on his successful career, during which Xi has duly practiced the loyalty and devotion of a Party member. Thirdly, he has remained loyal to the Party despite adversities. Xi's career has not been any smooth sailing. When his father was politically persecuted, he did not shift in his convictions because of his family's sufferings. Throughout his career, Xi has inscribed his loyalty to the Party in bone and blood, never doubting his faith or deviating from it under all circumstances. It is the loyalty to the Party that supports his convictions in the Party.

Second, CPC leaders must be open to self-improvement and faithful in their Party convictions. There is an end to one's career, but no end to one's convictions. Cultivation of firm convictions requires long periods of effort, even a lifetime of devotion, which is determined by the fact that commitment is enhanced through practice and tests. For Xi, there are mainly three methods to enhance his commitment to the Party. Firstly, his commitment grew through lessons and experience, which are indispensable for strengthening one's ideals and convictions. Like he said, to consolidate the beliefs that "only socialism can save China," "communist ideals are great," and "becoming an outstanding Party member," one must learn from facts and experience and go through difficulties and adversity. This process is evident from his forced exile to the countryside and his decision to go to Zhengding. It is through transformations like this that he examined his convictions and ideals with sound judgment, and after cycles of such examination and extraction, internalized the beliefs and applied them in work and life. Throughout his career, Xi has always upheld his beliefs and ideals, never shifting despite all forms of tests and challenges. Secondly, for Xi conscientiousness and convictions are the foundation of the Party, which should be strengthened through theoretical studies and self-cultivation. According to him, he is first and foremost a CPC member and his priority is to work for the Party. He has always paid attention to self-improvement and self-discipline, performing the duties of a Party member no matter what office he holds, and setting high standards for himself even in high office. His loyalty and devotion to the Party and its cause have made him a role model in safeguarding the CPC's image. Thirdly, Xi has lived a lifetime of devotion. He believes that one's convictions in the Party will not deepen on its own, nor will it be enhanced with promotion, but must be attained through a lifetime of devotion and hard work. To enhance his convictions in the Party, Xi spares no effort in learning from the people and from positive models, strengthening self-discipline and self-cultivation to remind himself of the importance of learning. He said, "We must often admonish and examine ourselves, setting strict standards for our actions, and conscientiously accept the supervision of the Party organizations and the people." This is a genuine depiction of his doing and the secret to strong belief lies in learning from others, from past lessons, and from conscientiously improving oneself.

Third, CPC leaders must take on responsibilities and become role models. Leading by example has been a time-honored tradition of the CPC and reflects the advanced nature of the Party. Xi has carried on the positive tradition by setting examples at various posts and proving the advanced nature of the Party with action. Drawing strength from revolutionary pioneers, setting positive examples with integrity and character, and pursuing the ideals of the Party, Xi stands at the frontline of the Party, holding the banner for all Party members. Born to a revolutionary family, Xi grew up in an environment that held heroes in high esteem, cultivating heroism in his young heart. When he was a child, his father was his biggest hero and the pride of the family. After he started working, Xi was greatly inspired by the story of the model CPC county committee secretary Jiao Yulu, by his firm beliefs and sacrifices for the people's well-being. One man is weak, but those who follow a great man's example could carry forth on the same path. Mao Zedong was also greatly respected by Xi, who commented on various occasions, "Mao Zedong is the pride of Shaoshan, of Hunan, of the Chinese people, and of the Chinese nation," and "We must not forget Mao Zedong Thought, otherwise we will lose our foundation." These remarks were proof of his ultimate respect for the older generations of Chinese revolutionaries. Xi believes that only by setting positive examples for lower levels can one govern with ease, a principle that he has always upheld throughout his career. In Zhengding, he visited all villages under the county's administration to implement the "six regulations;" in Ningde, he visited all nine counties within three months, riding a jeep into the depths of the muddy mountains; in Zhejiang, he visited 90 counties, cities, and districts in one year's time; in Shanghai, he visited 19 districts and counties in seven months; at the national leadership, he took the lead to implement the Eight Regulations and the Three Guidelines for Ethical Behavior and the Three Basic Rules of Conduct. All these not only reflect the political convictions of a CPC member, but have also set a positive model that has had a strong impact. Building the CPC into the greatest, most advanced, and most viable party is the key mission for Xi, a mission that he will always carry on with passion and devotion. From the Chinese Dream and the new round of reforms, we can see his aspiration for a strong Party and a strong country; from his sweeping campaign against corruption, we can see his strong will for the well-being of the Party and its growth; from his determination to fight foreign interference and domestic conspirators, and from his confidence in adhering to the Chinese path, we can see his commitment, his willpower, his principles, and his character. His leadership by example and pursuit of lofty goals has turned his convictions into steel, strong and firm. Since he took over, Xi has spared no effort in ensuring stability in China, wasting no time in solving the pressing problems inside the Party, curing chronic illnesses, setting up strict regulations, and implementing discipline. With great courage, he has pushed all-around reforms in the Party and the country, liberating and developing productive forces, and enhancing China's overall strength. He has carried out rigorous campaigns to regulate the army, cleansing it of bad influences, and ensuring the army operates under Party leadership and in service to the people. These reforms and overhauls truthfully reflect the strong convictions of Xi Jinping.

CHAPTER SEVEN

Setting Standards for Leadership Capabilities

Key Phrases

The value of setting standards for leadership capabilities is based on the following needs:

- The need to develop modern political science
- The need to understand the patterns of governance
- The need to strengthen the governing capacity
- The need to improve the abilities of officials
- The need to revitalize the Chinese nation

Around the world, there is a growing interest in studying the CPC and Xi Jinping. It is justified in a sense that interest in Xi reflects the interest in China today and its future. Xi's governance strategies and his successes have showcased China's ability to lead not only its own development, but also to contribute to global development in the future. Studying Xi's governance philosophies and understanding his leadership capabilities goes beyond the usual publicity effort, but it's based on the needs to explore the path of Chinese socialism and the CPC's governance, to modernize China's governing system and governing capacity, to enhance the country's hard power and soft power, and to promote the orderly and harmonious development of the world. As the leader of the CPC and the nation,

Xi is a symbol of the Party, the Chinese people and the nation. He is a man of the world. For people in China, studying his governance philosophies, leadership style, personal qualities, and leadership capabilities is not only conducive to deepening the understanding of his governance system, but also to implementing the CPC's guidelines and policies, and to promoting solidarity and concerted efforts. Following the example of Xi, Party officials at all levels will put in more effort to study and improve themselves, and a set of standards on leadership abilities will be developed in light of China's conditions. The standards should be easy to follow and examine, and should respond to the current needs. Targeted programs will be carried out to train industrious officials who are approved by the Party organization, loyal to the Party's cause, trusted by the people, and ready to take on responsibilities. This will not only strengthen China's official leadership team but will also contribute to the development of political science and the governance of officials around the world.

I. The Need to Develop Modern Political Science

Throughout history, the rise of a nation or an era was always empowered by strong leadership and outstanding leaders. During the Han Dynasty (202 BC-AD 220), Emperor Wu (156-87 BC) ushered in an era of prosperity, and Emperor Guangwu of the Eastern Han (5 BC—AD 57) also pushed powerful economic growth. All the golden eras of development in the Tang, Ming, and Qing dynasties were closely related to their wise emperors. Similarly, historically speaking, the Roman Empire, the worlds' strongest empire at the time, came into being because of Julius Caesar; Tsar Alexander II laid the foundation of Russia's prosperity in the second half of the 19th century; and great men like George Washington, Thomas Jefferson, and Franklin Roosevelt played an indispensable part in the rise of the United

States. History has proven that leading figures play a key role in determining their countries' destinies.

Around the world, political scientists mainly focus on the studies of political behaviors and systems, rather than on politicians themselves—there is yet to be systemic research in this regard. Theoretically, political science will not be complete without research on the politicians; in practice, neglect of the politicians' role in national development will lead to errors. Facts have proven that different degrees of development between similarly-structured countries are largely attributed to the disparities of their leaders' abilities, which can sometimes determine their countries' fate. To further develop political science, more effort should be made on the studies of politicians, so as to enrich and develop political science.

The CPC is the leading core of Chinese socialism, and past leaders, such as Mao Zedong, and current leaders, such as Xi Jinping, are the focus of this core. Xi's accomplishments since he took over the Party, the state, and the military have demonstrated the importance of having great leaders. He has many superb qualities: a good education and being well-versed in traditional culture, entrepreneurship, a broad vision, philosophical thinking, governance capabilities, and charisma, firm convictions, selflessness and righteousness, patriotism and care for the people, endurance and tenacity in pursuit, planning and holistic approaches, the courage to face challenges and take on responsibilities, self-cultivation and self-improvement, which are all part of his leadership capabilities. Those leadership capabilities are an integration of political belief, governing ability, innovative spirit, and integrity and character required of leading figures, and have set new standards for leadership. Understanding his governance strategies, and Chinese leaders' growth and development, will contribute to political and leadership studies around the world.

II. The Need to Understand the Patterns of Governance

The revitalization of the Chinese nation on the path of socialism is a historical mission of the CPC. Over 60 years ago, during his talk with Mao Zedong, Veteran educator Huang Yan-pei summarized that just as a political party or a country could thrive quickly, it could also decline in an instant. Huang said that in the beginning everyone is hardworking, everything is addressed with caution, so the country prospers; but in the end, when people stop working, demise is not far behind. This pattern has applied to every dynasty. Historically, almost all feudal dynasties lasted from several decades to no more than three centuries, when the imbalances between productive forces and productive relations and between economic base and superstructure led to the decline of old regimes and the rise of new ones. This pattern continued into modern times—the Soviet Union collapsed several decades after it was founded.

To break the pattern and reduce its influence, kings and emperors had taken great precautions and countermeasures. Some especially ambitious politicians had enough foresight to push revolutionary reforms, which had effectively delayed the fall of their regimes. In 140 BC, when Liu Che, Emperor Wu of Han, ascended the throne, the Han Dynasty was over 60 years old, with plenty of wealth after years of development. Yet many problems were rising, such as the difficulties between the central government and localities, and between the weakened central authorities and powerful local warlords, rising ethnic contradictions, and menaces from the Xiongnu nomadic people. The emperor was faced with the choice between conservative governance and taking proactive measures when the country was able to. Emperor Wu made a wise choice and set the goals of his rule. He took a series of effective measures to reform the court, expanded territory, fought off the Xiongnu, opened up the Silk

Road, and ushered in the first golden era of Chinese history. It was difficult to keep the status quo, but even more difficult to take new ground. Following the call of the times and bravely accepting the challenge, Emperor Wu is now remembered as a great leader who, during his 54 years of rule, made China one of the strongest countries in the world. After his reign, Western Han continued for another 96 years. Without him, the history of Western Han could have been completely different.

China has come to a critical juncture. A strong China has walked out of a humiliating history of modern times, emerging as a new power in the world with a thriving economy. After six decades of development, it is undeniable that China's society still has many complications, and the CPC still faces major tests. The grand goals need arduous efforts to be realized, and the path to a bright future is always rugged. On this new starting point, if China wants to break the periodic pattern of regime change, it will need a reformist-leader who has the political courage to innovate, and to lead Chinese socialism to new heights. Facts have shown Xi Jinping is the right leader for China. He has bravely carried on the historical mission of the CPC to revitalize the country and the Chinese nation.

Therefore, studying Xi's governance philosophies and his core capabilities answers the strategic need to understand the CPC's governing pattern. The objectives are: first, to uncover the laws and patterns behind governance and better understand the CPC's governing pattern; second, with Xi as an example, to reaffirm the Party and the people's convictions in the CPC; third, through studying Xi's governing strategies, to better understand and implement national guidelines and policies. With a correct understanding of the central role of leading figures, the new generation of CPC leadership will steer the giant ship of China to fare torrents and waves, break through obstacles, and sail to victory.

III. The Need to Strengthen the Governing Capacity

The special nature of the capabilities of leaders determines that capabilities are closely linked to the ruling party's governing capabilities, and occupy an important position in the national governance system.

First, governing capabilities play a leading role in modernizing the governance system and governing abilities. For any political party, the governing capabilities take center stage of their party building, because a lack of governing capabilities will lead to the party's downfall, which will result in the change of governments. This is why enhancing governing capabilities must always be a priority, so as to modernize the governance system and governing abilities.

Second, the modernization of the governance system and governing abilities is an indicator of a party's governing capabilities—the higher the capabilities, the stronger the party is. To effectively strengthen the governing abilities, there need to be concrete programs, and modernizing the governance system and the governing abilities is a key medium. Therefore, the governance system and governing capabilities are irreplaceable in demonstrating a party's governing abilities. Improvement in the governing abilities is largely reflected in the modernization of governance system and governing capabilities. In China, the purpose of understanding leaders' capabilities is to summarize the effective ways to enhance the CPC's governing abilities through studying Xi's governance philosophies and strategies.

Third, the capabilities and governing abilities of leaders are the foundation of modernizing national governance capabilities. The capacities of ruling parties and state leaders play a key role in modernizing the governance system and the governing abilities. There is no exception for any political party or nation to enhance their governing abilities. They must rely on organization, the institutions, and the officials. Compared with the traditional "national administration," national governance has entered a higher level with enriched content, varied subjects, and comprehensive goals, which requires a capable team of officials to be up to the task of modernizing governance. Officials at all levels must have the capacities to support the initiative to modernize the governance system and governing abilities, otherwise modernization will lose its momentum. Without leaders' essential capabilities as the base, governing abilities will lose the roots and reduce the efficiency of the governance system.

It must be pointed out that the efforts to interpret Xi Jinping's governance philosophies have been fragmented, without systemic research, which cannot keep up with China's improvement in governance. A complete, precise, systemic, and research-based interpretation is urgently needed. Focusing on studying the leadership capabilities of Xi will help better understand his governance philosophies at the theoretical level; conducting comprehensive studies of Xi's achievements, governing strategies, essential capabilities, and development tracks will lead to all-round understanding of his person; and summarizing the governing philosophies, guidelines, and strategies of Xi's will ensure a systemic and more objective understanding of him. There is no doubt that the efforts will go beyond ordinary research on politicians, and beyond a "how to be successful" handbook. It will not only help the CPC and the people reaffirm their convictions and commitment in the Party's ideals, improve their understanding of China's development path, and solve the difficult issues of development and push reforms, but it will also unite the mind and action of the Party and the people under the guidance of Xi's governance philosophies, so as to modernize the governance system and abilities.

IV. The Need to Improve the Abilities of Officials

When examples and standards are set, people follow. The standards for examining and evaluating officials embody the values of an organization. Despite the CPC's attention to building a high-level team of officials, breakthroughs are yet to be made on key matters due to the sensitivity of reform, and more efforts must be made to innovate the selection and cultivation mechanism for officials. At this crucial time of transformation, China is facing a myriad of problems, which are posing great challenges to the leadership. Old methods no longer work, new methods are still alien to most, tough measures are too harsh to use, and soft measures cannot solve problems. These are all blockading reform. Therefore, training and selecting capable officials has become an urgent matter. The capabilities behind Xi's governance philosophies have set good standards for training officials in the new era. Since 2000, the author has done extensive research on three questions: What are good officials like in the new era? How to select good officials through effective means? How to train good officials? The author went on to develop a theoretical framework based on the capabilities, centered on comprehensive examination and evaluation, and targeted at higher efficiency of officials' training, contributing to the research on the topic.

As time changes and different circumstances arise, people are putting more emphasis on officials' awareness of their duties, their abilities, and performance, and the criteria for evaluating officials have also changed. The practice of officials' governance has demonstrated that despite differences in style, great leaders have four aspects in common. First, they have conscientiousness in carrying out responsibilities, good understanding of the correct political and development direction, and unique vision and foresight; second, they have competency in decision-making, coordination, and control, clear work methods, efficiency, and outstanding work capabilities; third, they have an open mind, industriousness, and the courage to tackle problems, to innovate and reform, and to blaze new trails; fourth, they have integrity and character, self-discipline and self-cultivation, leading by example, and other personal qualities. These are what we call "core capabilities." In summary, these capabilities of leaders include the capability to perform political duties by holding to the correct political direction, the capacity to perform official duties by promoting development, the capacity to enhance innovation by promoting reforms, and the capacity to lead by example by strengthening self-cultivation and self-discipline. Chinese leaders' capabilities include political discernment, work impetus, innovative drive, and self-improvement. These four core abilities have carried on the CPC's requirements for its officials in terms of integrity, ability, diligence, performance, and clean governance, and have integrated the new requirements for officials. Under in-depth and specific principles on officials' governance, they reflect the Party's nature and mission, its goals and tasks, regulations and discipline, and requirements on conduct, with major progress in innovation based on fine traditions. The proposition of the core capabilities have made the qualities of leading officials more direct, clear, and specific, a response to the development in the new era. These capabilities also have their basis in history and in the people. Since ancient times, the Chinese have always respected officials who are loyal, capable, diligent, and honest. Those who are loyal, but not capable are not accepted by the people; those who are capable, but not loyal are not liked by the people; those who are diligent but not honest are not trusted by the people; and those who are honest but not diligent are not supported by the people. People today have the same requirements for officials, who must be loyal to the Party's cause, have what it takes to perform their duties, courage to tackle difficult issues, and discipline themselves with high standards. Only in this way can they win the people's respect and support.

Xi Jinping has set the standards for cultivating the core capabilities of leadership. All leading officials shall follow his standards and learn from him, and action should be taken to promote these standards Party-wide. In the meantime, efforts should be made to extend and enrich the standards, to build the core capabilities of leading China's development at all levels, and to explore a path of enhancing these capabilities by examination and evaluation, so that true talent can stand out and govern their localities to better effect. All these will lay the solid organizational foundation for modernizing the governance system and the governing abilities, and for realizing the Chinese Dream.

V. The Need to Revitalize the Chinese Nation

History is a mirror that reflects the rise and fall of empires. In Chinese history, important dynasties had all valued leadership building, and all the historical periods of peace and prosperity were directly linked to wise leaderships. The prosperity of the Han Dynasty owed to Zhang Liang, Han Xin, and Xiao He's contribution; Emperor Taizong of Tang was supported by his capable court officials Fang Xuanling, Du Ruhui, and Wei Zheng, for example. History has repeatedly proven that only with good leadership can a country or a political party ensure stability, peace, and prosperity. Otherwise, if the leadership is weak in belief and incompetent in governance, it will only lead the nation into oblivion. Over 90 years of CPC governance has proven that the key to successes in revolution, construction, reform, and development lies in the Party and the governing team.

A capable leader needs a capable team. To realize the Chinese Dream of the rejuvenation of the nation, the country needs a wise helmsman to guide the way and the support of leading officials to navigate the seas. Since CPC's 18th National Congress, the new generation of CPC leadership has been paying equal attention to promoting Party conduct, and strengthening officials' abilities. The modernization of the governance system and abilities has been made a main goal of the reform, which requires officials to have corresponding abilities. Today, China is faced with complicated situations domestically and internationally, while the CPC is facing severe challenges and the people are asking for better performance of officials. With Xi's leading capabilities as an example, the Party must expedite the steps to train officials who are firm in belief, dare to take action, fear no difficulties, and improve themselves with strict discipline; to bring up officials who start from grassroots levels, understand the people, know the national conditions, and are good at tackling tough issues; to train officials who have sound theoretical bases, are competent, and uphold honesty and integrity; to identify officials who are confident in the path of Chinese socialism, its theories, and system, and who practice what they preach; and to select officials who are truly capable of performing their duties, taking concrete action, and keeping close ties with the people. In a word, the Party must bring forward more officials with capabilities.

Realizing the Chinese Dream is the biggest goal of China. To realize the Two Centenary Goals, the CPC must rely on officials at all levels to lead the people towards the goals. The Chinese Dream embodies the mission of the Chinese people to revitalize their country and shoulder the aspiration of the people for the future, a daunting task in every sense. Therefore, officials under CPC leadership must wholeheartedly embrace the Chinese Dream, and enhance their capacities to lead the people in realizing this dream. Under new circumstances, establishing the standards of governing capabilities based on Xi's capabilities, and guiding, evaluating, and training officials in accordance with Xi's capabilities are conducive to improving the leadership abilities of officials at all levels, to selecting real talents who are capable of leading their localities to prosperity, to attracting talents from all sectors in order to modernize the governance system and the governing abilities, and to lay a solid organizational basis for realizing the Chinese Dream.

On a broad sea we sail, the wind saying bon voyage. The giant ship of China has set sail, onto the great journey of revitalizing the Chinese nation. Realizing the Chinese Dream requires firm political convictions and extraordinary wisdom, and the governing abilities and planning of great leaders, and the strong support and hard work of the people. There is reason to believe that with Xi Jinping—a wise, capable, visionary, and firm leader—as captain, the Chinese ship will definitely reach its destination despite all forms of difficulties.

POSTSCRIPT

———————

There is an ideal which kindles a fire early in life and burns for a lifetime. There is a calling which hits the notes early in life and resonates for a lifetime.

I was born in southern Jiangsu Province, a place abounding with great statesmen and scholars since ancient times. As a young boy, I made up my mind to be useful to my country, an ideal inspired by famous people such as Xu Pu, a respected minister in the Ming Dynasty, Zhou Peiyuan, renowned physicist and scientist of the 20th century, and Xu Beihong, a great painter and arts educator of the modern era. My ideal was practical—to change my life and my poor hometown through hard work. As I grew older and learned more, especially with the knowledge of modern China's humiliating history, I began to understand only a strong nation can bring stability and prosperity to individuals. I used to wander off to the Grand Canal, look up at the sky, and pondered on these questions: How is such a big country governed? What kind of person can be its leader? Looking back, those questions sowed the seeds for my interest in state affairs which led to more in-depth thinking. Once sowed, the sprout never stopped growing.

As a young man I began to read history, trying to unveil the patterns of the rise and fall of dynasties, and learn from great leaders' merits. It gradually became clear that behind every power, there was always a strong steersman with superb abilities. These great men include Julius Caesar who ushered in the golden age of the Roman Empire, Franklin Roosevelt who saved the United States in the depths of the Great Depression, and Mao Zedong who led the Chinese people toward national liberation. Then I knew—the key to national development lies in the people, in the leader.

Fate brought me closer to the topic. After I left the army and began working in personnel management, my main duties were to implement the Party and state policies on selecting and training officials, which gave me the opportunity to further my studies on the topic. Throughout my career, knowing more about good officials, their performance, and their growth, I discovered that they have something in common to support them, which plays a central role in their development and successes. If we could summarize and promote these qualities in officials, we might find a new way to enhance officials' performance, and through their role, ensure stability and bring about prosperity in the nation.

Since 2000, I studied the common qualities of great leaders in an effort to uncover the patterns behind their successes. Inspired by the concept of core competitiveness, I named the common traits of great leaders "core capabilities." For 15 years I have published theoretical works such as *Core Capability of Leaders—Exploration and Practice of Chinese State-Owned Enterprises, Examination and Evaluation of the Core Capabilities of SOE Leaders, Core Capabilities—107 Questions on Developing the Ability to Lead,* and *Support the Chinese Dream with Core Capabilities.* I was the first in China to propose the concept of leaders' core capabilities, establishing the theoretical framework of core leadership capabilities, opening a new area of research on leadership, and offering a new perspective, a new way of thinking, and a new path to the selection and use of officials.

After the CPC held its 18th National Congress, its leadership headed by Xi Jinping took over the responsibility to steer

China through complicated situations domestically and internationally. It began to lead the Chinese people to make headway in the building of a moderately prosperous society in all respects and in realizing the Chinese Dream, instilling vitality into the Party and the nation, and bringing hope to the people. The strong leadership of Xi in managing internal and foreign affairs, in addressing the deep-rooted problems of reform and development, in planning for the country's future, and in mustering the strength of the Chinese people dawned on me as the perfect example of a great leader, with every core capacity required of him.

The great 20th century writer Lu Xun once said, "Greatness needs to be understood." Xi and his governance philosophies should be understood, implemented, and followed by more people, and there should be someone to summarize and showcase the strengths of his philosophies, qualities, and values. That was when I had the idea to write a book on his governance capabilities. When it began, however, I ran into great difficulties. It was difficult because it was a new area without precedent knowledge; because it was hard to grasp the essence of his philosophies due to his short time in office; because I did not have the opportunity to observe him close-up; and because my busy schedule kept me from allocating more time to think and research. Most difficult of all, nonetheless, was that the research object involved the leader of the Party and state, and the topics were often sensitive. All of these called for my confidence in the task, rigorous research methods, and logical thinking and phrasing. Despite the difficulties, I pursued my goal with great determination and did not give in to the daunting difficulties.

This is a powerful calling, an inexhaustible strength—the calling from the deeply-buried seed from childhood, the strength from the patriotic soul that has only grown stronger. In a year's time, supported by this powerful calling, I wholeheartedly devoted myself to the reading and research on President Xi's published speeches and writings, using whatever time available to me to think and write. The sleepless nights and countless revisions witnessed the birth of my brainchild. It is indeed a short book compared to other works in the core capacity series, but due to the special nature of the research subject and the topic, and the difficulty of the research itself, the book bears significant meaning for me and is my pride. It is my genuine hope that through this book, readers could get a full picture of President Xi's governance strategies, and of the depths of his philosophies and capacities. It would be my greatest honor if this book contributes to modernizing the governance system and the governing capabilities, and to realizing the Chinese Dream.

Finally, my gratitude goes to everyone who has lent their encouragement, help, and support, without which this book would not have been finished. Experts from the Party Literature Research Center of the CPC Central Committee, the School of the CPC Central Committee, and the National Defense University of the People's Liberation Army provided their valuable opinions on the draft. Mr. Fu Chengyu, member of the Standing Committee of the Chinese People's Political Consultative Conference and former chair of Sinopec Group, was very supportive and wrote the foreword for the book. My thanks also go to my publishers, the Publishing House of the School of the CPC Central Committee and Sinolingua, and the aforementioned persons and organizations who have given their valuable support. I am open to comments and criticism from all sectors and walks of life.

Zhou Xinmin
February 26, 2016